A Complete Life

A Complete Life

DISCOVERING YOUR AUTHENTIC SELF

PAUL HUDON

A Conscious Shift Publication
Conscious Shift Publishing Registered Offices: Saint Petersburg, FL 33710

2022 Paul Hudon
Library of Congress Control Number: 2022900289

Print: 978-0-9995960-6-7
ePUB: 978-0-9995960-7-4
Kindle: 978-0-9995960-7-4

Author Paul Hudon
A Complete Life: Discovering Your Authentic Self/Paul Hudon

Published in the United States of America

Cover Design: Elisa Tanaka
Front Cover Photo: Paul Hudon
Interior sun graphic: bagus_pangestu for BigStock
Digital version produced by BookNook.Biz

This book is creative nonfiction. The information and events in this book are the experiences and ideas of the author. The ideas in this book have been expressed and written as remembered by the author.

For more information on how to purchase this book or to schedule the author for speaking engagements please contact the author directly at
paulhudonauthor@gmail.com or
Conscious Shift Publishing at ConsciousShiftPublishing.com.

To my lovely wife Jane,
whose inspiration and encouragement
have made our journey together
a wonderful experience.

Table of Contents

Preface

I have always had a desire to understand the outside world, as well as the inner world within. I believe there is much more to our experience on Earth than just our physical being. Because of this belief, I began the journey to discover a deeper connection, one few people around me understood. I wasn't even sure what a deeper connection meant, though I knew I would know it if it found me. Meditation, and writing in a journal became a daily practice. It was here I discovered that what I was seeking was within me the entire time.

Little did I know the journey would connect me with my authentic self. This may sound odd, yet I discovered a part of myself previously unknown to me. This part of me was a voice that spoke to me with love, kindness, and compassion. I call this voice my Inner Voice. I have learned that I can ask my Inner Voice questions and receive loving answers. This book is a dialogue between me, and the loving guidance I receive from my Inner Voice. You'll note throughout that the questions I ask myself are in italics while the corresponding responses are from my inner voice.

What does a dialogue with my Inner Voice mean? If all things are energy—thoughts, words, and actions—then my Inner Voice is energy as well. This energy comes to me in the form of a voice. To write these conversations, I quiet my mind and then listen for this powerful but kind, loving voice. The words flow easily if I am focused and centered. If for some reason I lose concentration, I retrace what I have written until I pick up the flow again. This way I receive the full meaning and intention behind the words.

As I wrote this book, I was amazed by the depth of love and compassion I felt. In all my conversations, I have always been guided to ask the right questions and seek the topics most beneficial for my well-being. I have never felt ashamed asking a question that may have seemed out of place. The answer was always given with love and kindness. If for some reason I did not fully grasp the meaning of the answer, there was a thorough explanation, so I had a complete understanding of the intention behind the answer.

The chapters in this book are subjects that came to me during my daily writing. As I wrote each morning, asking questions as I usually do, these subjects felt powerful enough for me to seek more clarity.

Through these conversations I have learned much about myself, and the lessons that are revealed from past experiences. I know for me; the learning has only begun. With each new page and each additional subject I write, my awareness of how the world affects me is heightened, as well as how I affect the world.

I feel honored to share this book with people who are looking to find the wisdom within themselves. My journey started with wanting more connection to my work. As it turned out, I became more connected to my life, which has been a wonderful experience.

As you read this book, let yourself be guided to what feels true and right for you. Allow the topics to settle within, before moving on to the next page or chapter. Give yourself time for reflection, or to write a thought in a journal. Life is a journey; contemplation benefits the flow of life on this journey.

My hope is you enjoy this book as much as I enjoyed writing it. I also hope this book helps you find the connection you are seeking in this lifetime.

Peace, Paul

Introduction

Do you know of the tremendous love found within you? How often have you looked to other people for lasting love? Is their love authentic? Is their love true and honest? The love within you is everlasting, meaning it never wavers or falters, no matter how difficult life may become. This book is about finding the tremendous love within you, as you discover your authentic self, and begin to live a complete life.

The author's ability to quiet his mind allows him to hear a gentle voice, which he calls his Inner Voice. This voice is the eternal energy of love. The author translates this energy in to words—much the same way your instincts are interpreted as guidance. His trust in this loving energy has grown with many conversations and written pages. He can experience these conversations any time, as long as he is centered and focused. The love and truth he feels while engaged in a conversation has allowed him to experience life in a way that was once unknown to him.

Love is the basis of positive energy; it is this love that is the foundation of this book. Because of this love the author shares the wisdom he has learned through conversations with his Inner Voice.

Eternal, loving energy has been called Spirit, Source, The Great Creator, and God. Trust that love flows to all people no matter what they choose to call this energy.

While reading this book you will notice subjects not commonly discussed. Each subject is given a chapter of its own, which allows the subject to be explored with depth and meaning. As you read further you may notice a common thread. Love. Love for yourself, and love for those in your life—love connects all of the chapters. This common thread also benefits you on your journey.

This book has been written with love, kindness, and compassion. The intention is for you to discover the love within you, and then begin a new way of living by experiencing a complete life.

BEGIN WITH JUDGING YOURSELF AS WORTHY.

Judgement

Few words generate the same strong reaction as the word "judgement." Whether it is the judgement of others, or the judgement of yourself, either will ignite a powerful emotional reaction. How often do you judge your neighbors or yourself without realizing the impact of your judgement? Are you using your false beliefs as the foundation of your judgement? Is your judgement a benchmark to validate your self-worth? These topics may cause an emotional response within you just by reading the word judgement and thinking of how painful it can feel to be judged by others.

If judgement is too strong a word, the word "compare" could be used. How do you compare yourself to those around you? Do you have a need to judge yourself against those you work with? How does this make you feel when you compare yourself with the people you went to school with? Do you compare the relationships in your family with those in your neighborhood? These are some of the ways judgement is harmful.

Judgement may also be used as a gauge to mark your progress. Whether it is a personal goal in sales, sports, the arts, or anything in which you measure yourself against another person.

You also judge yourself against who you think you should be. This is where judgement may be destructive to your well-being and those in your life.

In an act of judgment, you are claiming to have more knowledge about a person or subject than others. There may be times you state your judgement as fact that should not be disputed. Yet, no person knows what another person has experienced, or is currently going through. Nor can a person honestly know what you are going through at any time in your life. They could guess, but they would be wrong. If someone claims to know your life experience, you may become uncomfortable, get defensive or upset. It is the same way with your judgement of another person, judging them based on what little you truly know. When you say to yourself, "They should…" in doing so you are ignoring what they have gone through to get to where they are in life and instead replacing it with your experiences. You are making this statement based on your knowledge, not theirs.

Look at these examples. If there is a person in your town who appears to be homeless, what do you feel when you see this person? What do you say to yourself as you pass them on the street? How do you judge them in comparison to your life experiences? Here is another example. Your neighbor next door has a child who has the attention of the local sheriff. How do you judge your neighbor's parenting skills against yours? Finally, the neighbor across the street has a loving, caring family, unlike yours or any other you have seen. How do you judge yourself against such a family? You may also judge yourself harshly because you have not accomplished what the neighbor across the street appears to have accomplished. Can you see how you may judge others based on your life experiences? In all these examples, there is judgement founded on a lack of realistic understanding of the situations and those involved.

All people, including yourself, are doing the best they can at any given moment. If you say they could be doing better, then you are judging them based on what little you know about their life. The person who appears to be homeless may be doing better at handling their life now than they have in their past. You don't know. Your judgement of them is based on a small amount of information. It is unrealistic to get an honest evaluation of a person's life as you pass by them in the car. Imagine someone judging you after you had a rough day at work. You may want to shout out, "I had a bad day, I'm not always this way." Yet it is too late, you have been judged on that brief moment. Other people do not have all the information about your day, just as you do not have all the information regarding the person who appears to be homeless.

In the world in which you live, there is tremendous diversity in all things—people, art, religious beliefs, to name just a few. There are endless amounts of differences on the planet. It is this diversity that makes traveling to foreign locations and meeting new people exciting. These differences are what make your interactions wonderful. It is also the diversity that causes you to judge others wrongly, even though you may lack an understanding of their situation.

Perhaps a family from a foreign country moves in next door and they are slowly learning English, maybe too slowly for you. Yet you may judge them because they speak their native language at home, eat uncommon food, and wear different clothes. Until you get to know your neighbors, you are judging them with the limited information you have.

Imagine your job takes you to a foreign country where your native language is not commonly spoken. You are not suddenly stupid because you are unfamiliar with the language and customs of this country. So, too, it is with your neighbors. They do not want to be judged because you do not know their language. Nor do you want to be judged throughout your life. These examples show you how often you may judge others based on how they appear on the surface.

All people feel and experience love, compassion, and kindness. These traits have no boundaries. The emotions of love and kindness are spoken without words throughout the world. This is what you have in common with the people in your diverse neighborhood. All people have the ability to speak the emotions of love and compassion. There is no need for judgement if you choose to express these powerful emotions.

Though all people can feel the emotion of love without words, people also feel the negative emotions of judgement, as a parent, a life partner, even as a person. As you examine your life, you can see how you have judged yourself compared to others. Self-judgement is not rooted in self-love or compassion. This judgement is based on how you want other people to accept you. If you do not measure up to their expectations, you may judge yourself as unworthy.

Self-judgement can be emotionally damaging to you in ways you may never realize. With these negative thoughts, there is also negative energy flowing within you. Each word of self-judgement tells you you're not worthy of your inner self-love; not worthy of allowing yourself to grow from the mistakes you have made. There is not the acceptance that at this moment you are doing your best. Negative self-judgement is telling yourself you should be doing better, you could be a better person, or even a better parent. You never let up on yourself, always putting yourself down. These kinds of negative thoughts produce negative energy within the human body, which may cause illness and poor health.

The words of self-judgement are more powerful than the negative words other people speak to you. This is because you can tune out the voices of these people. It may be difficult to suppress the negative judgement you constantly repeat to yourself. Self-judgement comes from believing the negative things you have learned to accept about yourself. These are false beliefs. Negative thoughts and words can have tremendous impact on your life. By repeating a negative belief to yourself, it can gain so much strength it may begin to shape the way you experience the world.

With little focus you may recognize some of the things you judge about yourself. However, it is beneficial to focus on the things that make you so perfectly different than anyone else. Only you can place value on your self-worth. There is no need to give this responsibility to other people because they do not know your authentic self. This is where self-judgement is the most damaging to you physically and emotionally. You must take the responsibility for your own happiness back from other people to begin to experience the tremendous love within you. No matter what other people say or think about you, begin with judging yourself as worthy of the everlasting self-love found within you.

I'm thinking of how self-judgement is so damaging to people. Is there a root cause for self-judgement?

There is a desire in all people to be loved by those around them. This desire may cause you to change your behavior to suit the needs of those in your life. When you feel you are not meeting the expectations of those whose love you seek, you judge yourself as incapable of receiving their love, thereby changing your behavior to fit their needs. This cycle may continue for years, always judging yourself, then adjusting your own behavior in the hope that at some point you will receive the love you have been dreaming of. This behavior separates you from your inner guidance and your inner self-love. You have been placing the desire for love from another person, ahead of discovering your love for yourself.

To be loved by others is a powerful desire. Don't all people want to be loved by those around them?

If your desire to be loved by others falls short, and you judge yourself as unworthy, you are perpetuating an unsustainable way of life. You cannot maintain a healthy, loving life if you are always telling yourself, you do not measure up. The uncertainty you feel behaving this way is telling you you're not connected to the voice within that only speaks of its love for you.

In finding the value of your self-worth and self-love, you are able to enjoy lasting, loving relationships. To change who you are to please other people is judging yourself against the standards of those in your life. Experiencing your inner self-love will be your new standard for your self-worth. This may lead you to a life without self-judgement, or the need to judge others.

I'm using the standards of other people to judge myself unfairly?

As you desire the approval of those around you, you use their standards and beliefs as a measure of your self-worth. In doing so you have placed their opinions of who they think you are in a higher regard than your true beliefs about yourself. If you did not have the desire to please others as a way to boost your self-worth, you would not have to judge yourself or change who you are to seek their approval.

How do I judge myself based on the opinions of others, rather than judging myself on my true beliefs?

People may not be aware of their true beliefs, because they have been judged by themselves and others for years. True beliefs can be silenced by the constant stream of negative self-talk that goes along with self-judgement. Once you recognize the reasons for your self-judgement, you may begin to change these habits to ones more in line with what you know to be right for you. Negative self-talk is a powerful force of judgement. You can break this pattern by focusing on what makes you unique and self-loving, without seeking the approval of those around you.

Won't people judge me if I tell them I love myself?

Would you prefer to stay in a situation where the opinions of other people are more important than the opinions you have toward yourself? Or would you rather value your own opinions based on self-love and self-compassion? You will be in a more positive, emotional state of mind when you do not need their approval to elevate your self-esteem and you are no longer subjected to their judgement.

It seems so natural to judge others and ourselves. Isn't that how we gauge our progress?

There is no need to gauge yourself against anyone for any reason. The true gauge is how you are feeling and experiencing life based on your self-love. Your happiness should never be compared with that of another person because their life experience is different than yours. Even within a family, your experiences will be different than those of your parents or siblings. To compare your life to the lives of others is to judge them, as well as yourself. Whether you call it compare, gauge, or judge, it is unfair to you and those in your life.

The measure of your success, or improvement, is determined by your increased awareness of your inner self-love, and the joy you experience throughout your day. The depth of your happiness will be an accurate indication of your success.

I could argue my happiness doesn't pay the rent.

You could argue that, yet you are underestimating the power of your happiness. You are implying that paying the rent is more of a priority than your happiness. Judging your life this way is placing your needs for inner love as a lower priority than the rent. You are unwilling to see the other side of the judgement coin, yet you are unable to move to a better place emotionally, because of this false belief.

If you were to seek your own happiness without self-judgement, you would be guided to all you desire. You would always be moving in the direction that makes you the most joyful, as well as the most satisfied with who you are. From this place of joy, your rent will be easy to pay as you live a fulfilling life.

I'm beginning to understand that self-judgement is self-defeating.

As you judge yourself, you are telling yourself you are not good enough, creating a defeatist attitude within you. You are basically saying you are not worthy of living a complete life.

Is it possible for other people to tell if they are being judged, even though nothing is said?

The energy of your emotions, thoughts, and judgement, radiate out from you and are felt by all those you encounter. If you are silently judging someone, this energy will be felt by those you are judging. Look over your life. You may remember a time you felt this silent judgement. When you become aware of the energy your thoughts and words radiate, you can choose to stop this form of judgement.

As with feeling love from another person, so, too, can you feel the negative energy of anger. Judgement is no different. Those you are judging feel this negative emotion radiating from you.

Toss a pebble in to a pond, the ripples fan out from a single point. Your emotions act the same way, radiating out from you, affecting everyone you come in contact with each day. While in judgement, whether you are focused on one person, or a group of people, they will feel the powerful energy of your judgement.

Even if I am not speaking the words of judgement, the intention can be felt by those I am silently judging?

Few people realize the power of the energy they radiate. Every thought and word releases energy, this energy is felt by all people and beings on Earth. Whether these are the thoughts of love and compassion, or anger and judgement, this energy is felt by others.

Why is it so easy to judge other people?

It is easy to judge others because oftentimes it makes you feel better about yourself. If you knew what the other person has experienced in their life, it is likely you would be more compassionate with your words and thoughts toward those you judge. Judgement comes from a lack of true understanding of a person's life experience. You are basing your judgement on incomplete information.

I can look back and see times in my past when I judged someone, only to be surprised at how wrong I was. Why was the lesson so powerful?

Your eyes were too clouded by judgement to see the potential of this person. You judged them incapable of the task they set out to accomplish. When they surprised you after accomplishing the task, you felt uncomfortable because you knew you judged them harshly and unfairly. The unsettled feeling within you was the disconnection between you and your inner self-love. When you judge others, you lose touch with the pure love that is your truth. This separation is revealed to you by unpleasant feelings.

If I judge other people, I'll continue having these unpleasant feelings?

If you stop judging yourself and others, you will not have to experience these unpleasant feelings. Judgement is a powerful negative emotion. You cannot judge someone, without experiencing the uncomfortable feelings surrounding the negativity of judgement. Your judgement of other people is based on little true information. Once you see the real person, you will recognize how wrong you were about them.

I know myself better than anyone, doesn't my self-judgement have merit?

Many times, self-judgement is harsh and condescending. Even if you are comparing yourself against other people, you do so to make yourself feel better. Judging yourself is saying you are not worthy of a better life. You may be saying that to yourself anyway. This type of self-destructive behavior prevents you from experiencing the love within you.

How do I grow emotionally and become a better person if I do not compare myself to those around me?

There is no positive growth judging yourself against another person because you are either judging yourself as inadequate, or superior to them. There can only be lasting growth when you allow your inner self-love to guide you to the best life possible. If you change your behavior to satisfy your negative self-judgement, there will not be positive growth. This cycle of negative self-judgement may continue until there is little accomplished that has any lasting meaning.

Releasing the desire to compare yourself with those in your life sets you free to experience a life of self-love and self-compassion. You may make mistakes, yet the intention is to learn from these lessons in a loving way. If you are not happy with your life, negative self-talk from the act of judgement will not produce any long-lasting benefits.

Does self-judgement affect my health?

While you are judging yourself, you are telling yourself you are not worthy of experiencing a healthier life. You are wasting your time and energy by putting yourself down, instead of appreciating who you are, what you have, and what makes you truly unique. Self-judgement does not allow your inner love to guide you to what is honest and right for you -- whether it is a better job or improved health.

If there is a constant stream of negative self-talk you are not hearing the guidance advising you to eat better, go for a walk after work, or any loving advice that recommends taking care of yourself. In a sense, you are making yourself feel bad for not doing more for a healthier life. With this frame of mind, it may be hard to find the enthusiasm to seek a better life.

In the constant act of self-judgement, you may begin to believe there are no good solutions to improve your current situation. With this limited mindset it can be a difficult process to find your footing, and then move to a healthier place emotionally.

Won't I be constantly judging myself anyway?

Release the need to judge yourself against the standards of your culture. Instead, gauge your life experience by the loving guidance your emotions speak to you. It is always beneficial to work toward better feeling emotions. These feelings guide you to a place of joy and happiness. No other person has the right to tell you if you are happy. It is your responsibility to learn your inner truth. This way of experiencing life is more truthful to who you are.

There is no reason to compare yourself to other people because their happiness will be different from your happiness. As you release this need for self-judgement, you allow yourself to experience your self-love, and self-compassion. In the process, you regain your self-worth, while seeing your happiness improve. You no longer have the need to compare yourself with others.

What about envy? This seems to be a common emotion? Does envy fit in to this conversation?

The emotion of envy is telling you your circumstances do not have value. Also, you would rather experience the life someone else is living. You are judging your current situation as unworthy of your effort, wishing for something better. To envy is to rob yourself of your self-love, attempting to find what you are seeking elsewhere instead of finding it within yourself.

If I envy someone with money, am I judging myself as unworthy of the wealth or the love within me?

You are saying another person has a better life than you because of their money. This is also an act of judgement. You are judging them only on the basis of money, not on the complete happiness all people are meant to live. When you envy someone with money, you are saying to yourself you are less of a person because you do not have as much money as they do.

What another person has may never make you happy. Your happiness will be found within you, not in your bank account. The money may help, but if having money is your definition of happiness and true self-love, then you may never be happy because you may never have enough money. If you stop judging yourself against other people and then discover the pure love within you, you will not need an endless amount of money to make you happy. You will have found within you a flow of love that never runs dry, no matter what the economy does.

What happens if I release the need for judgement or envy?

When you release your need to judge or envy others, you come face to face with the truth of who you are, by experiencing your own self-love. In this connection you recognize your self-worth and the powerful truth that you are doing your best at all times in your life. As a result of this state of mind, you begin to express love and compassion to those you encounter in your day. Whether you speak through words, thoughts, or emotions, you will be radiating love and kindness out to the world.

COURAGE IS YOUR POWERFUL INNER STRENGTH.

Courage

When the word "courage" is spoken, you may think of a firefighter entering a burning building, a soldier walking through an abandoned village, or a teacher explaining world events. These honorable examples of courage come to mind, while countless others go unseen.

The intention is to explore courage on a more subtle, personal level. The courage within you to pursue your passions, your well-being, your self-love, and the strength to be your true self. This degree of courage is no less admirable than the courage of the firefighter or soldier, though just as necessary to live a complete life. Courage is found within all people, it is there for the asking, yet oftentimes you fail to tap into this reservoir of courage. Learn to trust your own courage to guide you to a life that exceeds your expectations.

Your courage gives you the strength to know what is right for you by how the thought of it makes you feel. Having the courage to trust yourself allows you to make the right decisions, at the right time. With your increased awareness of your courage, you begin to realize you do not need the opinions of other people to direct your life. You will have the courage to make your own choices based on what is true and right for you, giving you the strength to stand up to those who doubt your decisions and question your actions. No person knows you as well as you know yourself. It is your life after all. If your decisions make you feel a level of joy and love you have not felt in the past, then these are the right choices. Because of these authentic choices you now have the courage to follow through with your decisions.

Courage is your powerful inner strength. Look within to find your courage and the loving energy of who you truly are. You may have false beliefs or the voice of negative self-talk hindering your ability to experience your courage. Fear may also be involved when accepting your courage when you fear you may fail. So why try anyway? You may have an increased level of uncertainty because of what other people will think if you start something new. Courage comes from recognizing you are worthy of the tremendous love within you and this love carries you through the challenges of life. There is no need to fear this love. You have the courage to allow yourself the right to experience your own self-love.

Courage gives you the strength needed to silence the negative voices constantly speaking in your mind, clearing the way for your inner voice of self-love to become the dominant voice. You might feel badly after a person berates you. In a case like this your self-love gives you the courage and the strength to say, “Stop!” You can then begin the process of changing your life to one that is more self-loving and compassionate. Courage is self-love and self-love is courage. Because of your willingness to experience your self-love, you will receive the benefits of courage to help move you to a more centered state emotionally.

The strength to discover your true self has a foundation of courage. You do not have to look for courage if your desire is for a better life. Just by asking for a healthier situation, you have opened the door to experiencing this powerful source of courage.

Why is it so hard to find the courage needed to change our lives?

When you attempt something new and fail, you may fear being ridiculed by others. This can increase your fear of failure and cause you to hesitate when a new opportunity presents itself. Life changes take time and courage. At first it may be easier to change the small things in your life. This allows the momentum to build as you gain confidence in your courage. From your success you begin to feel your courage build. You can then move on to more challenging aspects of your life. If the desire is there for a positive life change, the courage will be there to support you.

If that is the case, why do people fail at life changes?

Your life changes may come at a time when you are not focused on a positive frame of mind. If you quit a job while you are angry, you must first resolve your anger before a better job comes your way. If not, you will find yourself in a similar situation as you were at your previous job. With each life change there are lessons to learn. If you quickly move from one unsatisfying job to another, there will be little time for you to improve your emotional state of mind. You are too involved in the negative emotions of your past job to feel any guidance that would benefit you in finding a new job. Taking the time to get yourself in to a better place emotionally takes courage. Yet the courage is to your advantage because it adds positive strength to your desire for an improved situation.

Why is it certain aspects of my life don't make me feel very courageous?

There may be many challenges in a person's life. Within these challenges are lessons you are meant to learn. In these lessons you find the courage needed to face similar challenges in the future. When you are not feeling courageous, it may be because there are false beliefs you keep repeating to yourself. These false beliefs prevent you from hearing your inner voice of self-love. Having the courage to work through your false beliefs, to experience who you truly are, allows you to feel more courageous in the future. Staying positive in challenging situations now becomes the way you experience the world around you.

Should I have strong positive beliefs about all aspects of my life?

As you gain courage in trusting who you are, you also gain confidence in all aspects of your life. With more confidence there will no longer be areas of your life you are uncertain about.

Why is that?

Courage allows you to ask yourself any question and then trust the answer that feels best. Have the courage to ask for guidance first of all, then wait to feel the answer. This is where the belief in your courage is most beneficial. If you ask a question and you do not have any trust in the answer, you will miss the guidance giving you the courage you are seeking. In this case, having the courage to trust what your emotions are telling you will be an advantage in all your decisions.

Why do I need courage to trust myself with the decisions I make?

At times you second-guess yourself. There are also people who question your decisions. This places tremendous pressure on you to answer a question or behave in a certain way, possibly to gain the approval of others. Staying true to who you are is where your inner courage is the most important. Only you know what makes you happy and joyful. Having the courage to follow your path will prove to you you're making the right decisions based on your inner trust.

Why do I need courage to face the people who doubt me?

The people around you may be unaware of their own inner voice that is always speaking to them through love and compassion. If someone is doubting you, they are judging you based on their life experiences, not what is best for you. Their doubt may come from having little understanding of who you are, or what you have experienced in your life. It may take courage to face those who doubt you yet recognize that knowing what is true and right for you will do more for you than anyone's doubt.

Is doubt the opposite of courage?

They are not opposites. Doubt creeps in when your courage begins to fade. Self-doubt is a signal to look within and tap in to the strength of your self-love as a way to bolster your courage and confidence.

Why does it take so much courage to live in this day and age?

Today, tremendous knowledge is accessible within seconds. Some of this knowledge is beneficial to your experience, and some is not. Your inner courage allows you to feel what is right for you, and then learn to trust what your emotions are telling you. This courage may help you stand up for yourself against those who doubt you, or it may give you the confidence to make critical, life-changing decisions. Courage also gives you the strength to discover the truth of who you are and then to live authentically by this truth.

It takes courage to discover who I am?

The world around you is constantly trying to change you in different ways. Remaining true to yourself takes inner strength and courage. Your life is your journey, no one can walk the path of your truth for you.

Countless people change who they are to please the world around them, yet they would benefit from courageously discovering who they are. Any judgement they may have about themselves is because they lack the courage to realize their true selves.

Does it take courage to see people for who they are now and not how we remember them in the past?

To see people for who they are now means you have released them from the box you placed them in when you judged them. You now see them with a fresh understanding of who they are today. Think about how you have changed over the past few years. Other people have changed as well.

All people want to be seen for who they are in the present moment. It takes courage to let go of any judgement or false beliefs you may have toward others. Finding the courage to be open and learning something new about them, without judgement or prejudice benefits you, and your relationship with them.

Some people are challenging to be around. What then?

It is up to you to find the courage to accept them for who they are. All people are connected to the love that has created all things. Seeing challenging people through this love may take some courage. Yet wouldn't you rather be seen in the eyes of love as opposed to the eyes of judgement and ridicule? Being around difficult people may take courage, but your courage allows them to be themselves, as you remain true to yourself.

There is a reason you know these challenging people; they are teaching you lessons you need to learn. It may take courage to silence your negative opinion of them and look within yourself to learn these lessons. Once the lessons are learned you will have less judgement toward them and begin seeing them as teachers. The awareness of seeing challenging people as teachers helps you along your journey to discovering a complete life.

Why do some things in my life require more courage than others?

Not all experiences in life require the same level of courage. Dealing with your bank account takes a different level of courage than dealing with an uncooperative coworker. The things requiring a strong degree of courage are lessons you are meant to learn. The more important the lesson, the more strength and courage needed to understand the lesson. Once you learn the lesson, you will have an awareness that all the people and experiences in your life are teaching you something important. It may be easier to accept challenging people and situations if you are courageous enough to see them as potential learning experiences.

I'm beginning to understand that in challenging situations there are lessons for me to learn, but I have to be courageous enough to see through the challenge to recognize the lesson clearly?

In challenging situations there are lessons that are beneficial to you. If you approach these situations from a place of fear and negativity, you will have an experience that will justify your fear and negativity. In a courageous state of mind however, you may experience something that makes you uncomfortable, yet you are aware of the potential lessons you may need to learn at the time. Once you have learned the lesson, the challenging situation loses much of its strength, and you begin to enjoy more inner peace.

Having the courage to stay in a positive frame of mind when things are not going well, allows me to see the lessons?

Having the courage to maintain a positive frame of mind in a challenging situation will show you the strength and trust you have gained in your ability to remain true to yourself. There may be nothing you can do to resolve the situation, but you can maintain a positive mindset, founded on your inner courage.

It does take courage to stay in a good frame of mind, because it is possible to easily slip in to the negativity of the experience. This makes it harder for you to return to a place of center and courage. If you remain in a good, positive state of mind when events in your life get challenging, you have learned important lessons.

What happens when I realize I can't maintain my courage any longer?

When you lose the ability to be courageous, accept that up to a point you were doing the best you could at staying strong and focused. Be kind to yourself if this happens. This is not the time to abuse yourself for losing strength. No good can come from this self-defeating behavior. Accept that you have been doing the best you could, and trust that in a short amount of time you will have the strength and courage to carry on.

You do not have to be so courageous you feel you must carry the burden of the world on your shoulders. If the burden you carry is heavy, be courageous enough to ask for help. Then search for the inner guidance that feels best and move in that direction.

Why is asking for help so difficult?

People believe when they ask for help, others think of them as weak or incapable. Appearing weak is not a trait people want to portray. It is likely you do not ask for help because you believe the opinions of other people matter to your self-worth. You want to appear stronger than you are to maintain their positive opinion of you.

The hope is other people see you as strong because their opinions of you are how you value yourself. You would rather break from the burden, than appear weak by asking others for help.

Your true self-value is found in discovering your inner courage. From this point on, the opinions of other people no longer affect how you view yourself. Your strength gives you the courage to hear your inner voice constantly speaking its love for you. Because of your inner courage you can ask for help without it impacting your self-worth.

I lack the inner courage to ask for help because I do not want to appear weak in the eyes of those around me?

In failing to ask for help, you teach yourself you are unworthy of your own self-love. Your courage is nowhere to be seen because you are afraid of what others think. The desire to appear strong in the eyes of others is a powerful need.

People also believe that by asking for help it creates a burden on others, thinking it is better to handle these challenges alone. The belief is other people have problems of their own and do not need to be bothered by a call for help. In a true state of self-love, you would help them if they asked you, and you would do so without judgement or criticism. If you need help, those around you may be too busy to notice what is happening in your life. Love yourself and courageously ask for help, if they say no, move on without feeling any rejection.

It's interesting how it's self-loving to ask for help instead of it being a sign of weakness.

It is courageous to ask for anything you want in your life—a better job, a better car, even a loving life partner. If it is a true desire, then courage is needed to allow these things in to your life. Weakness is not a word that should be used to describe anyone at any time. Knowing that all people are doing the best they can at any given moment prevents a loving and truthful person from ridiculing or judging others. When you are aware of your self-love, inner strength, and courage, you recognize the love within all people, even if they may not appear to be at their best when they come in to your life. This type of understanding takes love and courage.

Why does it take courage to speak out against the negative things other people are saying and doing?

It can be easy to remain silent without much thought as to how your silence affects the world. The question to ask yourself is, how does remaining silent make you feel? To stay true to yourself, true to your inner love, takes courage. It is this courage guiding you when to speak up or not. To live a complete life is to speak your truth no matter what others are saying or doing. Your truth is founded in love and this love radiates out to the world around you.

Is it possible to be courageous for someone else?

You can be an example of courage for those in your life. By your example you help boost their own sense of courage. When your courage is honest and true, you radiate courage to those in need. If you are trying to be courageous and it is not an honest emotion, those near you are going to feel this emotion as confusion, causing uncertainty within them. There is no point in trying to hide an honest emotion, you radiate the energy of the emotion you are experiencing. Attempting to hide your emotions, only causes uncertainty within you and those in your life. This will cause them to feel more insecure than if you were expressing your true emotions.

Why does it take courage to express my true emotions?

Your emotions may not be what others want to hear, or they may not care what you are experiencing. Expressing your true emotions does take courage because you may have to choose between remaining true to yourself or staying silent as a way to please others. If you choose to be true to yourself, you will appreciate the courage needed to speak your truth without the fear of what others may think. Speaking your truth changes the way the world sees you. People will know who you are without having to sift through the mixed emotions that occur when you are trying to hide your feelings.

How do I handle the changes that can occur if speaking my true emotions changes my relationships?

Speaking your true emotions with courage and integrity reveals to others the truth of who you are. If speaking your truth changes your relationships, then your relationships have not been based on truth and honesty. Your relationships may change, but they will change for the better as you become more honest with what you are expressing in your words and actions.

Do I have to speak my truth? I'd rather not have to find new friends.

When you are courageous enough to speak your truth with honesty, you open yourself to the tremendous possibilities that only appear while living your authentic life. Your words radiate energy. It is this energy your friends feel. If you are speaking your truth the energy of your words is felt on a subtle level. You have felt it when someone close to you is not speaking honestly with you. Those around you feel the energy of your thoughts and emotions as well. Trust that as you begin to speak with honesty and courage your life will change in positive ways. Your friends may change, yet you may become an example for them as you begin to speak your truth.

I never thought my life could change by courageously speaking my truth?

If your life changes drastically, it is because you have started to speak and live your authentic self. From this awareness, you are able to see how disconnected you may have been from your inner honesty.

When you begin to speak your truth, you will have discovered what is true and right for you, and then you begin to live by this truth. While in this place of self-acceptance you can trust what you are feeling, trusting the guidance of your emotions, then being courageous enough to trust your inner voice. It takes courage to be honest with yourself. Yet from these powerful truths the world will treat you with the same level of honesty as you honestly treat the world.

Courage is needed for most aspects of a person's life. Is there anything I have missed in this conversation?

The courage to forgive others, as well as to forgive yourself. The act of forgiveness gives you the strength to release yourself from the burden of a past hurt or negative experience. The courage to forgive comes from the desire for a healthier life. Forgiveness is encouraged because it clears the way for you to see the path ahead, without the cloud of fear or judgement.

People believe that to forgive they must come face to face with the person who caused their pain. This is not the case. As you work to forgive those in your life, you will experience a flood of love within you that has been blocked by these negative experiences. If your desire is for an honest, loving, and compassionate life, then you also have the courage to forgive those in your life and to forgive yourself.

I need courage to forgive myself?

Self-forgiveness is an important act of self-love. Having the courage to forgive yourself means you accept who you are at this moment in time. You can then forgive yourself for the self-abuse that comes from believing you have made mistakes in your life or believing the false belief that you could have done better. These acts of forgiveness toward yourself are powerful acts of self-love. Courage is needed because you may have to defend yourself from the negative self-talk you keep repeating to yourself. In a sense, your courage is essential to preventing you from believing the negative things people say about you, as well as the negative things you may believe about yourself. When you turn your courage within, you release an endless flow of love that has always been within you. With courage you can enjoy this love and fulfill your desire for a complete life.

My courage comes from a desire for a better life experience?

If it is your intention to live a more self-loving life, you will find the courage to accomplish this. Courage is within all people, all that is needed to experience this courage is to have the belief your true desires are possible. Within this belief to live a better life, is the energy that has created all you see around you and the love found deep within you.

It's courageous to love myself?

From an early age you have been taught beliefs that may not be true about you. If you hear these words long enough, you may begin to believe what you have been told. It takes courage to sift through these beliefs and begin to understand who you are. Throughout this examination, you will discover the inner self-love that has always been within you, and you can begin to enjoy this love. Your courage builds as you become more familiar with what makes you truly happy. To discover the truth of who you are, is to have the courage to allow yourself to live a life filled with joy, love, and true happiness.

IS THE BELIEF FOUNDED IN LOVE, OR NOT?

False Beliefs

What is a false belief? How do false beliefs affect your life? Where do false beliefs originate? To answer these questions, consider a few examples: the moon is made of cheese, the earth is flat, and you are unworthy of a wonderful life. Science has proven the first two examples to be false. These are false beliefs. Yet the last example must be proven wrong by you, even though you may believe it to be true. Everyone is worthy of a wonderful life experience, including you! And everyone carries false beliefs within themselves as well.

False beliefs are beliefs that are untrue, yet for some reason you believe them. Often, you add strength to your false beliefs because you continue to repeat them to yourself. You may have accepted these beliefs to be true because of a recent failure or a negative comment made by a friend or loved one. False beliefs also originate at an early age. As a child you believed those around you because you loved and trusted them. You had no reason to question if what they were saying to you was true or not. You may also believe what others say about the world around them—even believing what they say about themselves.

A false belief can be handed down within a family as well. These types of false beliefs have a tremendous amount of strength, having been discussed and reinforced for generations. "Our family has always been poor, and no one makes it out of this neighborhood," or, "No one in our family ever graduates from college."

These types of beliefs may become so strong they become part of the family's reality. It is the same way with your false beliefs. You accept these beliefs without question, and in doing so they become part of who you are. Breaking free from these kinds of false beliefs can be challenging.

How do you know if a belief is false or not? The answer is rather simple, you know from how the belief makes you feel when you repeat it to yourself. Is the belief founded in love or not? "I am unworthy of a wonderful life experience." Repeat this to yourself. Do you feel any love while repeating this statement? Can you feel the inner discomfort, as if someone inside of you is shouting, "NO! Do Not Believe This!" Why? Because deep within, you know this statement is untrue, yet for some reason you believe it. With any beliefs in a person's life, a continued focus on them adds strength to the belief. The more attention you give a false belief, the more control the belief has over your life.

When you become aware of the power of your words, you begin to understand how a casual comment can add strength to a false belief someone else is carrying. If you were to say to someone, "You are worthless," this could be the proof they are looking for to validate their false beliefs. When a person is in a vulnerable state of mind, they seek comfort from those around them. The nature of your response could either support them or reinforce their false beliefs. This is another way false beliefs are created; they are taught by other people.

False beliefs have no basis in the truth, they are created out of negativity and a disregard for what is honest, true, and loving. People of authority, teachers, doctors, grandparents, and parents can also add strength to false beliefs. You assume people of authority are speaking honestly, yet what they are saying may make you uncomfortable. This discomfort is telling you whether the belief is true or not.

Do all people have false beliefs?

All people carry false beliefs within their awareness. These false beliefs can, and often do, create the way life is experienced. Your false beliefs affect you, as well as the lives of those around you. People are naturally trusting. This makes it easy for a false belief to grow in strength and become the basis of a person's life. You can add strength to someone's false beliefs by how you act and speak. A false belief can be taught to those around you, and you can learn a false belief by what other people say.

I can add strength to someone's false belief, including my own?

It is not hard to add strength to a false belief, whether it is yours or that of someone else. Pay attention to the thoughts you think and the words you speak. These actions, if they go unquestioned, add momentum to a false belief. Reinforcing a negative self-image can increase the strength of the false belief a person carries within them. This belief could damage their self-worth. There are false beliefs society places on you as well, often without your complete awareness. If you are feeling insecure, or have a lack of self-worth, there is much you experience in a day that can reinforce a false belief.

Do people create false beliefs using the standards of other people?

Measuring your life experience against the life of someone else could cause you to feel inadequate, thereby adding strength to a false belief. The only real measure of your value, your self-worth, is the true love you have toward yourself. The word "true" is used because to live a complete life is to release the beliefs that do not serve your higher good from your consciousness. You then begin to experience who you truly are, while living a life based on self-love and self-compassion.

How will I know if a belief is true, or not?

There are aspects of your life that bring you great joy and a feeling of deep love. These activities are rooted in a true belief. This could be an emotional place you turn to when you are in need of comfort from the uncertainties of life. You may also be carrying other beliefs that are not true or founded in love.

For example, you may feel true to yourself when you are creating art or feel self-love while pursuing a passion. These are founded in a true belief. Yet you may have been told you are a terrible artist, or your passion has no merit. These beliefs are coming from an opinion someone has expressed to you. You know their belief about your passion is untrue by how much love and joy you feel while engaged in your passion. This is their false belief of who you are, not yours. Learning to tell the difference between a true or a false belief allows you to clear false beliefs from your consciousness.

The level of love and truth you experience while focused on a belief tells you if the belief is true or not. No person can honestly tell you what is right for you, only you know this truth. Releasing false beliefs allows you to enjoy who you are meant to be, without the need to judge yourself based on the beliefs of others.

Some false beliefs are easy to ignore, these are the ones you know to be untrue, yet for some reason you continue to maintain them in your consciousness. As you become aware of your thoughts and your reactions to the events in your life, you will know which false beliefs you can quickly discard.

I can release my minor false beliefs, but what about those having a bigger impact on my life? How do I identify the false beliefs I have been carrying within me for years?

It is beneficial for you to focus on how you feel as you repeat a belief to yourself. Whether it is true or not, you will have an emotional reaction. This emotional reaction is the feeling of love felt deep within you if the belief is true and right. This is your insight in to the belief in question. If someone says you are a terrible artist, there is going to be a surface reaction of defending your love of art. There will also be a deep response within you, telling you how much joy and happiness you receive while creating art. The latter example is how you tell whether your beliefs are true. As you become more aware of these deep emotions, you begin to recognize these feelings as guidance, helping you decide if your beliefs are true for you. Your true self is founded on love and compassion. When you believe anything other than this, you are accepting a belief that is not true for you, or anyone else.

If my true self is love and compassion, why don't I feel worthy of this love?

For most people, their self-worth is based on the false beliefs of the people close to them. They believe if other people treat them well, they have value. Conversely, if others treat them poorly, they feel rejected by those they hoped would maintain their sense of self-worth. People falsely believe their happiness is found in the opinions of other people. This is why you do not feel worthy of your own inner love and compassion. You have left the responsibility for your self-love in the hands of other people. Believing you are unworthy of your self-love is a false belief. Nothing is further from the truth. You came in to your physical body knowing of this inner love. As time passed you have replaced this knowing with the false beliefs other people have taught you.

I want other people to like me, why is that a false belief?

If you are seeking the approval of others as a measure of your self-worth, this is placing an unnecessary burden on them. In a way, you are asking them to provide you with the validation you need to be happy. Believing others will maintain your happiness is a powerful false belief, because no person but you has the ability to make you truly happy and joyful.

When you discover your true self-love and self-worth, you release those in your life from having to supply this love for you. You can experience your inner love without the need for their approval. With this feeling of self-love, you will be open to meeting new people who will allow you to speak your truth, without the burden of false beliefs.

Is it possible to create a life based on my false beliefs?

You can, and people often do, create a life founded on their false beliefs. There are people who do not recognize their life has been built on a foundation of untruths. Their lives may be fine to them, however there is much more to a person's life than the beliefs they have been taught by others. Oftentimes false beliefs prevent a person from living a complete life. To create a life, with true meaning and purpose, the beliefs not founded in love must be questioned and released from your consciousness.

Many talented people have—at one time or another—been told they have no talent. Those who do not believe these words, go on to become successful at their respective talents. If you believe you are untalented, you may be placing the beliefs of other people in a higher regard than the beliefs you have about yourself. There is no truth in a false belief, nor in the negative opinions of other people. No person knows you as well as you do. You will know your truth by the love and joy you feel as you repeat the belief to yourself.

The people who loved and raised me may have taught me some of my false beliefs?

There are people who do not understand the impact of the words they say to a child or to themselves for that matter. The false beliefs of others can have a tremendous impact on who you become as an adult, even though these beliefs may not be based on any facts. It is the trust in those who raised you that causes you to believe what they say.

When you were a child, you may not have trusted what you knew to be true for you because you had no way to prove or disprove what was being said to you. Your only clue may have been the discomfort you felt, but this may not have given you the insight to question what was being said. Questioning a false belief makes you aware of how a false belief is carried in your consciousness throughout your life.

If false beliefs have shaped my life, will I be speaking and advising those around me through these beliefs?

This is how false beliefs get carried down through generations. Each person believes the false belief to be true, and then the belief shapes the way their life unfolds. They will then be teaching others from their false beliefs. This is the potential impact of not questioning a false belief, or how a belief grows in strength when continued focus is placed on it.

I can have an untrue belief about myself and add strength to it by my continued focus on the belief?

If you are honest with yourself as you repeat a false belief you will feel an emotional response. If you are aware of what you are feeling, you may feel some uncertainty within you. This discomfort is telling you the belief is not true for you. Fill in the blank with any derogatory word, "I am ________." How does that make you feel? You notice how saying untrue negative words about yourself makes you feel uncomfortable. It is this kind of feeling you are looking for as you evaluate your beliefs.

Now say something about yourself you know is true and loving. Do you feel the difference? If you continue to focus on the false belief, you add strength to it, thereby affecting how you feel about yourself and how the world reacts to you. Repeating a positive, loving belief about yourself increases the strength of a positive belief as well.

Is it possible to have a positive false belief?

No, you cannot have a positive false belief. The nature of a false belief is one of a negative thought or experience. There is no love or truth in a false belief. You may be able to say positive things about your false belief, yet this does not make the false belief your truth.

False beliefs are not my truth?

Your truth is self-love and compassion, a knowing of who you are and what is right for you at all times. Your truth may be buried under layers of false beliefs and negative self-talk. However, it is easier to discern what your truth is while examining the emotions you feel when repeating your beliefs. If a belief is not rooted in love, then it is a false belief and should be discarded from your consciousness.

Can my self-image be based on my false beliefs?

All people want to be liked by others. This desire may cause you to change who you are to please these people. The desire to please others as a way to validate your self-worth, is a false belief. Pleasing others may only last for a short while, but eventually you realize you are not pleasing yourself. You falsely believe if you please those around you, you have value and self-worth. Your value and self-worth can only be found within you, without having to sacrifice your truth to find it. Your self-image and self-worth are established on a foundation of true self-love.

How do I reinforce a false belief in someone else?

Any negative words you say to someone have the potential to add strength to their false belief. As people look to those around them for advice or guidance, there is a belief they will hear an honest and truthful answer. The search for honesty is compromised when those giving advice are not speaking their truth. If this is the case, your negative intention has the potential to reinforce their false belief.

If I speak my truth, I may offend the person who is asking for guidance?

It is best to advise someone when you are speaking with love and compassion. There is no need to reinforce a false belief by keeping the truth from those who are seeking true guidance. If you believe they will be offended by you speaking your truth, then remaining silent may be the best course of action.

If the false belief of another person is powerful, should I try to set them straight?

It is best to speak your truth with love and compassion. Then from this place, it is easier to explain your views without being rude or adding to their false beliefs. They may then be able to recognize their own false beliefs. Your beliefs are true for you, but they may not be true for others. Although any belief founded in true, pure love will be true for everyone.

Is that only possible if I first recognize my own false beliefs, then release these beliefs from my consciousness?

You will know what your false beliefs are by how they make you feel. Releasing them from your consciousness allows you to experience your truth—the true you. It is this truth that encourages you to speak, and act through love, kindness, and compassion.

Is it up to each person to recognize their false beliefs and then work to release these beliefs to experience a complete life?

No person knows what another person is experiencing. Each individual has their own unique false beliefs based on their life situation. Even members of the same family may have different false beliefs that take different approaches to resolve. Yet to live an authentic life, false beliefs must be released from one's awareness.

What about the false beliefs passed down from generation to generation?

Each family member experiences the false belief differently than those around them. Even though they may have been taught the same false beliefs, family members have different life experiences. It is these differences that help shape how a belief is experienced. Each person will have a different emotional response to what they have been told—whether it is a true or false belief. By examining their emotional reactions to the belief, they will know if it is true and right for them.

Will I discover my inner truth by releasing my false beliefs?

False beliefs are emotional blocks preventing you from experiencing the truth of who you are. Even though you may be able to justify your false belief, it will hinder your ability to live by your inner truth. To recognize which beliefs to question, ask yourself if the belief has a foundation built on love. Not a love of power or the egocentric love people believe is associated with self-love, but a true, authentic love only to be found within you.

If you continue to focus on these false beliefs, you are blocking your ability to experience your inner truth. To realize your inner truth, learn what makes you loving, happy, and joyful on a deep personal level. Your inner truth never lies to you or leads you in a direction not right for you. This truth is your authentic strength which carries you throughout your life.

What about the false beliefs mankind has toward each other?

This is one of humanities biggest challenges, to release the false beliefs toward those who appear different. False beliefs hold people back from truly knowing each other. People have more in common with each other than they may be willing to accept. If you focus on your commonalities rather than your differences, you can begin to experience the inner love you have for your family, friends, and distant neighbors. This love is then spread to others around the world. Examine your false beliefs so you learn the true nature of who you are and the people around the world.

There are people who don't like me because of the country I am from. What then?

More people want to live in peace and harmony with you than there are who want to cause you harm. Focusing on the love you share with those around you is the best thing you can do for yourself and for the world population as a whole. Remember, false beliefs block people from experiencing the true, unconditional love available to them. False beliefs are not limited to only you, they affect all people, thereby hindering the ability to live in peace and harmony. Letting go of your false beliefs allows you to see people for who they are, and then to accept and experience their self-love as well.

To try to see the love within all people is a powerful thought.

It is no different than meeting new people in your neighborhood, you want to see the best in them, and you want them to see the best in you. There is no point in focusing on the negative aspects of people, because if this is what you are looking for then this is what you will find. You would like people to see you through the eyes of love and compassion, releasing the false beliefs they have toward you. Seeing through the eyes of love is the best way to effect a positive change within you, as well as those in your life and beyond.

If I release my false beliefs toward other people, will I become more accepting of them and our differences?

Having the courage to release a false belief helps prevent you from judging them as different. Sure, they may be different than you, but you now see these differences as unique and inspiring. Only then will you be more aware of what you have in common—which is love and compassion. With this awareness, you become more connected with the people you meet throughout your life.

What about their false beliefs toward me?

If you speak your truth—which is love and compassion—you show others who you truly are. This helps them release their false beliefs toward you. False beliefs are not based on facts, they are based on thoughts and ideas that have been taught to you. To help someone release their false beliefs of you, speak and live your truth of love and compassion. Their false beliefs are their responsibility to release. Your behavior either adds strength to their false belief or helps dismantle their false belief. The choice is yours.

It is surprising how powerful a false belief can be toward another person, even though we know little or nothing about them.

This type of false belief is based on judgement, and a lack of true knowledge about this person or group of people. The first time you see someone you may judge them on their appearance or how they speak. This initial judgement is not based on any long-term, truthful knowledge. Judgement of other people can create a powerful false belief. Even if you think you know this person, there is still the possibility you have a false belief toward them. This false belief will impact your interactions with them in a negative way.

Is my judgement toward another person a false belief?

You may not have accurate information about this person because your false belief is formed by a preconceived idea of who you think they are. To release your judgement of them is to accept that all people are doing their best at any given moment in their lives. If you believe anything negative about this person, you have judged them because of your false beliefs.

I don't think I'm doing the best I can. Is this a false belief?

This is a powerful false belief. However, it also reveals to you what you think about yourself. Based on what you know and how you are feeling at this time, you are doing the best you can. The false belief that you could be doing better than you are, is based on the feeling of not being good enough, judging yourself against an unrealistic standard. If you had more time, more information, or even better health, you would be doing your best at that time as well. There is no moment in your life when you are not doing the best you can. Any other belief about yourself is a false belief that shapes you and the world around you.

I'm always doing my best, always have been, and always will be doing my best? Some would say this is a false belief.

Return to the method of questioning a false belief. Is this belief rooted in love or the negativity of judgement? All people are doing their best at all times in their lives. Why do you keep repeating a false belief that does you no good? This belief is rooted in the myth that you do not deserve to love yourself. The realization that your inner love is always loving you no matter what false beliefs you have, will help you release these false beliefs. You may then experience your life with love, truth, and honesty.

At times I feel this inner love does not exist in my life. Is this a false belief as well?

This is also a powerful false belief. Your inner love is eternal, everlasting love. This love is always there for you no matter what you think or say about yourself. You are always being guided by your inner love, whether you accept it or not. This love is within you and has always been within you. Your false beliefs block your ability to feel and experience this powerful love.

Do all people block this inner love because of their false beliefs?

People deny themselves this love because of the false belief that they do not deserve this love. This belief may be so strong a person may spend their entire life attempting to find love everywhere but within themselves. To live a complete life is to recognize the endless flow of love within you, and then release these false beliefs from your consciousness.

What is the best way to release these false beliefs?

Learn to trust the infinite flow of love found within you. To welcome this love in to your life is to accept what is true for you by how you feel as you repeat the belief. At any given moment you are doing the best you can. This is the loving, compassionate way to accept yourself and to release any false beliefs you may have.

DISCOMFORT IS A WARNING THAT SOMETHING MUST CHANGE IN YOUR LIFE.

Comfort in Your Discomfort

The comfort in your discomfort, what is that about? What does that even mean? How is it possible to experience comfort in your discomfort? These are powerful questions, appropriate for a subject that has much to do with your emotional, physical, and spiritual health.

The question is, do you stay in situations that are not beneficial for you or are less than what you truly desire? People say finding comfort in an uncomfortable situation is desirable. Yet ask yourself, why do you remain at a job that makes you unhappy? Why do you maintain relationships that are not loving or kind? Most of all, do you settle for less because you are afraid of what challenges you may face if you pursue your true desires?

Could it be you do not feel worthy of a wonderful life? Is it because challenging yourself is frightening and threatening to your fragile foundation? Or is it because you have built a life based on your false beliefs, and as a result, you are unsure which choices to make for a healthier life? Do you choose to stay in an uncomfortable place where you may find comfort?

The comfort you find in your discomfort is an emotional decision, where you do not challenge yourself to live a more fulfilling life. In other words, you have chosen to stay in an uncomfortable situation because it is emotionally easier than moving forward. In this case, you have become comfortable in your discomfort.

There are reasons why people stay in uncomfortable circumstances: "I need the money," "I'm doing this for my family," or "Being with them is better than being alone," to mention a few. Even though people know what they want, and feel they deserve better, they choose to stay in situations that are unfulfilling. Why? Because oftentimes it is easier than changing.

Finding comfort in your discomfort means making the choice to stay in an uncomfortable situation because it seems like the right thing to do. Nothing that makes you uncomfortable or unhappy is the right thing to do. When you choose to remain unhappy you are telling yourself you are unworthy of the best life experiences possible. Sacrificing yourself for the job, the happiness of your partner or family, means staying in a comfort zone that will only cause you great discomfort in the long run.

Do you have the courage to look within yourself to find the reasons why you have chosen to remain in the comfort of your discomfort? Some of these reasons may be obvious, while others could be found in your false beliefs. When you choose to explore what it is that makes you truly happy—an inner happiness that cannot be found on the sale rack—you may begin to summon the courage to move onto a better way of life.

There may be times when you are unhappy or uncomfortable with your current circumstances. Ask yourself why you stay in a job or relationship that does not create a kind, loving and compassionate feeling within you. Staying in a place of emotional difficulty will in time begin to affect your emotional and physical health. In this uncomfortable place, you may begin to accept the negative self-talk flowing in your mind. As time progresses you may begin to believe this negative self-talk to the point at which you are too afraid to move forward, or to make any positive changes in your life.

One way to see if you are living within the comfort in your discomfort is to ask yourself if the life you are experiencing is true to your authentic desires? Have you wanted to move forward with new aspects of your life, yet have been too afraid to change for fear of the unknown? Even the fear of failure? Your growth comes from all your life experiences—successful or not. These experiences teach you to trust that only good can come from a positive life change. Staying within your discomfort means staying in one place and not moving forward with the intention of improving your self-worth or experiencing your inner self-love.

Are there ways to know if I am living the comfort of my discomfort?

Here are a few examples. You always use negative words to describe your job and although you are not happy, you do not look for another job. You are in a relationship that is not what you desire, yet you tell yourself being in the relationship is better than being alone. You choose to stay in an emotional or physical place that does not make you happy, and you are not seeking guidance to improve your situation. In these examples, you have chosen to stay in the discomfort of situations that do not make you happy. You know you are unhappy, yet you choose to stay where you are anyway. In behaving this way, you are telling yourself, you are unworthy of a fulfilling life.

By staying in a relationship or job that doesn't make me happy I'm telling myself I am unworthy of a healthier life?

This is what you are reinforcing each day you arrive at work or continue with an unsatisfying relationship. You are finding comfort in the discomfort of your choices. Also, you may be too afraid to move to a better place emotionally and take the risk of finding what is true for you. For your happiness, could you find the best job possible, without self-sacrifice, or experiencing any discomfort?

When you ask for a better job or life partner, you are saying to yourself you are worthy of a better life. You are telling yourself you want to experience the best life has to offer. Staying in an uncomfortable place, whether it is emotional or physical, is denying the self-love found within you.

Why would we choose to be in the comfort of our discomfort?

The life you are living is based on the choices you have made now and in your past. Whether it is a life partner, having children unexpectedly, or owning a poorly running car—these have all been choices. These types of choices can keep you in a life that does not make you happy. Being unhappy is a choice.

There is a false belief that you must sacrifice your desires for your family. Self-sacrifice is telling yourself you are not worthy of living the life you have imagined. This self-sacrifice will eventually cause you to experience some emotional unrest. If you choose to continue to sacrifice yourself for others, then you are accepting the decision to live your life separated from your inner truth.

You need a job, but why give up your desires, for a job that makes you miserable? You can change your life by pursuing your innermost desires, without sacrificing your happiness. Think for a moment. If you were to follow your desires, you would be happier, and you may even make more money. When you are happy, many unseen opportunities come your way, without having to settle for less.

What if I am afraid to find another job, move to a new city, or change my relationships? Things may not work out, what then?

If you continue to live in fear of failure, you have made the decision to stay where you are, even though it may make you unhappy. Being afraid of moving forward, is rooted in not trusting yourself to make the right decisions at the right time. All people have a loving inner voice guiding them all the time. Learning to hear this inner voice, and then trusting it enough to follow its guidance, will help you experience a better life. In doing so you leave the comfort of your discomfort behind.

You do not have to stay in an emotional situation that makes you unhappy. When you stay in your discomfort, you are settling for less than what you want. In a sense you are not giving yourself the support you need to improve your situation.

Change can be scary, at least I know what I'm up against where I am. So, why change?

Which is more threatening to you, staying in your discomfort, or moving forward toward a better life? In your desire for a healthier life, you begin to experience the self-love, and courage found within you. Because of this, you come face to face with your authentic self. Staying in your discomfort keeps you from experiencing the life you want to live. Learning to trust your inner guidance will be the way you are guided out of your discomfort and in to an awareness of self-love and self-compassion.

It seems I'm always unhappy, nothing is ever right, and my relationships never last. I don't like the way things are turning out. How can I be comfortable with this discomfort?

In the midst of the unhappiness you are experiencing, you are wanting a better life. Through your wanting, you are unaware or unaccustomed to hearing or feeling the guidance always flowing to you. Your inner guidance is loving, caring, and compassionate guidance, always directing you to exactly what you are wanting, if what you are wanting is true for you. It is your responsibility to accept that this loving guidance is flowing within you, and then to listen and follow this guidance.

Learning to trust what you are feeling before any situation allows you to know if the environment is right for you. There are people you meet who make you uneasy, this is guidance. In situations where you feel uncomfortable, this is guidance, attempting to guide you in a different direction. If you are aware of your intuition, you will feel an uncomfortable feeling before things become challenging.

When you speak of your relationships never working out, know that before the relationship started you may have been experiencing guidance which was steering you away from this relationship. It is your responsibility to listen for the guidance then follow this guidance for an improved experience.

You can ask for your life and relationships to work out better, but you must do something to make them work out. If you want a better job, yet you are not willing to improve your skills, then a better job may not be possible. It is the same way with relationships, along with all other aspects of your life.

I have to do something to move out of my discomfort?

In any job scenario, two things could happen. One would be you believe improving your skills is not necessary, you then move from one unfulfilling job to the next unfulfilling job, always staying in a place of dissatisfaction. Another possible option is to take a course to improve your skills, increasing your value to an employer, as well as bolstering your self-worth. From this improved situation, you begin to experience more self-love. With this awareness of self-love, you will move away from the uncomfortable circumstances that have been holding you back. The choice is yours, stay in an unsatisfying situation, or choose to do something to improve your options for a healthier life.

Is there a connection between self-love and the discomfort I often experience?

If you are feeling discomfort, you are not experiencing your self-love. Any discomfort you feel is there to show you that you have separated yourself from your source of self-love. Self-love is accepting that you have value to yourself and to those around you. Having self-love means realizing you are worthy of a better job, improved relationships, and an authentic life. Experiencing your self-love gives you the courage to move away from your discomfort to a more positive life experience.

Is it possible to live a life of self-love while staying in my unsatisfying job?

To live a self-loving life, you cannot live a life that makes you unhappy. Your self-love, and self-worth, always guide you to the life experiences that will lift you out of your discomfort. If you choose not to follow this loving guidance, it is possible you may fall back in to old patterns of being comfortable with your discomfort.

Do I have to change all aspects of my life to move out of my discomfort?

Think of these changes as small steps on a long journey. As you change certain aspects of your life, other areas will be easier to change. Begin by changing the parts that improve your life right away. Your attitude would be a good first step. If you change jobs with a poor attitude, before too long you will be experiencing the same mindset you had with your old job. This is true for all aspects of your life because your attitude helps shape the world around you.

As you change your attitude to one more self-loving and compassionate, you will experience a shift in how the world responds to you. In your awareness of your self-love, the courage needed for the improvements are found within you. Once you set in motion the desire to experience your self-worth and true self-love, you begin to move away from your discomfort to a more satisfying life.

What about the teachings of others that say I should find comfort in an uncomfortable situation?

To seek your own comfort in an uncomfortable situation is a way of allowing your feelings of self-love to be felt. It is vital to take care of your emotional needs first. If you are in an unpleasant situation, work toward finding a healthier emotional feeling. This does not mean to throw yourself in to the discomfort. It means to find emotional comfort in the situation. This will be the best thing for you. Once you place yourself in a healthy emotional state of mind it becomes easier for you to handle the uncomfortable situation. The actions and decisions you make will come from the inner calmness you have worked to achieve. Trust your inner self-love to guide you to the best thoughts and the right course of action in any uncomfortable situation.

Why is it so difficult to stay centered and act in a positive way when we get in to uncomfortable situations?

Staying centered is listening to your inner voice and then following its loving guidance. The difficulty arises when you focus on the uncomfortable situation and not on the guidance helping you in these circumstances. Often people allow themselves to get swept up in the negativity of a situation. They forget they have the power to remain centered and that they can move forward in a positive direction. Any decision you make with positive thoughts and actions benefits you more than if you were focused on the negativity of the discomfort. Acting with a more positive frame of mind gives you the strength and courage to seek out what is best for you in any challenging situation.

If I work to remain positive, will I have the strength to change my life and then free myself from my constant discomfort?

The strength to change your life originates with self-love and a positive frame of mind. As you begin this shift to a better way of living, you will enjoy more positive people and healthier situations coming in to your life. Joy and happiness cannot be experienced if you are in a constant state of negativity. Think of the times you wanted to be happy, yet you could not because you were too focused on the negative aspects of your life. This changes when you focus your energy on moving toward a better way of life.

Don't I grow emotionally from the negative experiences in life?

You grow because of the positive lessons found in negative experiences, as long as you do not allow the negativity to overtake you emotionally. When something unfavorable happens to people, they place much of their attention on the outcome and their resulting negative emotions. If they were to realize there is positive growth in all negative experiences, they would move to an improved emotional state of mind quicker. Thus, benefiting from the lessons found within the experience.

How does this affect my discomfort?

Any negative emotion, or the feeling of discomfort, is telling you there are things you must learn from this situation. These lessons may be to learn to trust yourself, or to increase your awareness of your inner self-love. Experiencing any discomfort means you are not following the guidance always being sent to you through your loving inner voice. Learning to recognize the lessons in negative experiences and trusting the guidance of your inner voice, gives you the strength to make the changes necessary to move away from your pattern of discomfort.

What do I need to learn from my pattern of seeking comfort in my discomfort?

There is much to learn from these emotional patterns. It is up to you to find the areas of your life needing your attention. If you look back over your past, you may notice a pattern of unsatisfying jobs or relationships that did not last. With an honest intention, look closely at these situations to uncover the reasons why these experiences did not work out. This is where true growth takes place. If your job makes you unhappy, there may be a pattern of choosing jobs that do not challenge you in one way or another. You may be getting bored, and this boredom causes a negative attitude along with poor job performance. The same may be true with your relationships. Are you settling for less because you do not want to be challenged with being true to yourself? These patterns, once realized, become opportunities to look within and release the fear which has created many of these patterns.

Discomfort is a warning that something must change in your life. There is no other way for you to know if you are on the right path other than to recognize the discomfort as an indicator to evaluate how you feel toward certain areas in your life. If you feel wonderful, happy, and loved, this is a signal you are headed in the right direction. On the other hand, if you feel discomfort, or any negative emotion, it is time to look at your life to see how you can move away from these negative patterns to a more positive experience.

The discomfort you feel when you think of your job, your friends, or where you live, is telling you it may be time to seek ways to relieve these patterns. If you are experiencing joy and happiness, this is good, you may not need to change anything. People often feel discomfort because of the negative experiences in their lives. They may choose to stay in negative situations, rather than challenge themselves to change their lives to a life that is healthier for them.

How does fear play a role in why people do not change to a healthier life experience?

Fear is a powerful negative emotion that can keep a person from moving in the direction they know is best for them. It may be easier to live with this fear, than to challenge their current situation. In this case their fear is more powerful than their desire to move away from their discomfort, thereby limiting their plans from ever being attempted or accomplished.

What are some of the ways to overcome the fear that prevents people from moving away from their discomfort?

Look within to discover the strength of your self-love and your inner guidance. These strengths are more powerful than fear, and when trusted, can lead you away from the negativity of your discomfort. With these new strengths there is no need to be afraid of failure because every potential setback is seen as an opportunity for positive growth. You may be apprehensive about what other people may think of your attempts to move past your discomfort. This can be overcome by slowly allowing your loving inner voice to guide you to what is true and right for you.

Many people confuse their loving inner voice with the negative self-talk they hear in their head. The guidance from your inner voice helping you move away from the comfort of your discomfort always has a firm foundation built on love, kindness, and compassion. Negative self-talk has none of these qualities. As you silence the negative chatter with a positive loving conversation with yourself, you also recognize when the opinions of those around you are not beneficial to your emotional health. Allowing yourself the comfort of your own self-love is the greatest gift you can give yourself. Realizing your true self-love will be the best way to move past your limiting fears and away from your discomfort.

How does negative self-talk cause fear within me?

A never-ending dialogue of negative self-talk causes you to constantly doubt and second-guess yourself. This thought pattern only increases the amount of inner fear you are dealing with. Because of this fear you are unable to move forward for fear of hearing the critical voice of negative self-talk over and over again. Negative self-talk is not who you are, this voice was born from self-doubt and the false beliefs of who you think you are. When you accept that negative self-talk can be silenced by your desire to move to an emotionally centered place, you will feel the courage build within you to put a stop to this self-abuse.

Why does negative self-talk have the ability to keep people in their discomfort?

People think their negative self-talk is their inner voice speaking words of truth. However, no true inner guidance is ever spoken that causes you to feel uncomfortable or advises you to do something not in your best interest. Negative self-talk is powerful because it creates a constant dialogue of self-abuse and self-doubt. If you have a desire for an improved life, it is best to stop the flow of negative self-talk, and then learn to trust the wisdom your inner voice speaks to you through your self-love.

Am I keeping myself in my own discomfort?

Often, people blame others for their circumstances. They fail to recognize or accept responsibility for how their lives have taken shape. When a person looks within themselves and realizes they have control over their discomfort, they can then begin the journey of seeking a better life. Once you notice you are keeping yourself in your own discomfort, you can make the positive changes necessary to move on to a healthier life, both emotionally and physically.

Once people recognize they have made a mistake, they often keep themselves in their discomfort by focusing on the mistake. How do we move away from this behavior?

If you are courageous enough to recognize mistakes as opportunities for positive growth, you learn to see these situations as beneficial learning experiences. With this awareness, it becomes easier to move forward with clarity and confidence. The choice to see mistakes as positive learning experiences allows you to release the need to criticize yourself, if things do not work out like you had planned.

What other reasons may keep a person in the comfort of their discomfort?

One powerful reason may be the false belief that self-sacrifice benefits those around you. In the long run, self-sacrifice causes an inner discomfort within you. You may be sacrificing your happiness for those who are not looking within themselves for their own self-love or are too afraid to search for their own true happiness. Sacrificing your true desires to please others may keep you in the same uncomfortable place for years. At some point this pattern will have a negative impact on your well-being. Through the act of self-sacrifice, you are allowing yourself to become unhappy. Your sacrifice may never make those around you happy either. Their happiness is their responsibility, just as your happiness is yours. Intentionally experiencing discomfort as a way to please others, is telling yourself you are not worthy of living a complete life.

The moment a situation or relationship begins to feel uncomfortable, recognize that the situation may not be right for you. This feeling is telling you that you may need to reevaluate where you are and why you are making the decisions you have chosen. With an honest evaluation of why you make the choices you do; you will have the tools needed to move away from situations or relationships that make you uncomfortable or are unsatisfying.

The choice is yours. Stay in your discomfort or summon the inner courage to move to a better place physically and emotionally. The solution to your discomfort will be found in your ability to love and trust yourself.

AT ANY GIVEN MOMENT YOU ARE
DOING YOUR BEST.

Doing the Best You Can

How often do you tell yourself you should be doing better? You could be improving your performance at work, having healthier relationships, or even being a better parent? Why is it difficult to accept that you are doing your best in every moment of your day? Are you judging yourself based on an unrealistic standard set by society? Do you compare yourself against what other people are doing, or where you could be at this stage of life if you just tried harder? Why are you so tough on yourself when you make a mistake at work, say the wrong thing to a friend, or burn the toast? Is it possible to accept the powerful truth that you are doing the best you can?

Look around. You will see plenty of messages in advertisements, books, even your friends and family, telling you that you could be doing better. It might be overwhelming if you consider the times people judge you as not good enough or tell you how to improve yourself in some way. Though this judgement may have good intentions, the advice can cause you to doubt and second-guess yourself, forcing you to delay or set aside your life dreams. Are you willing to accept that at any given moment you are doing your best, even if you find yourself in a place of confusion and hardship?

People judge you on how they think you should be handling the challenges you face every day, even though they may not have the full picture of what is happening in your life. If you believe the negative things others say about you, you could grow to be insecure and uncertain about the right direction for your life. Believing the negative opinions of others and constantly telling yourself you should be doing better, may cause you to doubt what you are capable of accomplishing. As you judge yourself for not being good enough, you are telling yourself you are unworthy of living a complete life.

If you could be doing better, you would be doing better, it is rather simple. Based on the knowledge you have at the time, the experiences you have had in your life, and the outside influences surrounding your choices, you are doing the best you can. Endlessly telling yourself you could be doing better is not going to make challenging situations any easier. Only you know what is happening in your life, and only you know the circumstances affecting your choices.

No other person understands your life or emotions as you do, and no person has the right to tell you how you should feel as you go about your day. They may think they know better than you, yet they do not. With the belief that you could be doing better, you can become stuck in a cycle of criticizing yourself through your negative self-talk. If you believe you are doing your best, you may have to defend your actions to those who judge you as not doing enough.

When you release your need for the approval of others, and silence your harsh self-judgement, you begin to understand that you are doing the best you can. It is in this awareness where you connect with your true self-love.

What does self-love have to do with doing the best I can?

Having a desire to be a better person, more accomplished with a skill, happier at work, or proficient with a hobby, are desires filled with self-love and compassion. When you express negative emotions toward yourself because you feel you are not good enough, is when you lack self-love. If your goal in life is to improve yourself in some way, you are moving in a positive direction. Yet if you criticize yourself for not being good enough, you are experiencing a lack of self-love.

How will I know if I'm doing my best?

The emotions you feel will be a signal if you are judging yourself fairly or not. Whether it is positive and loving, or negative and critical, these emotions tell you if you are being honest and true with yourself. You are always doing your best. You can learn to doubt yourself if you believe the negative opinions of others or live by the unhealthy standards of society.

When you accept that you are doing the best you can, you release the self-judgement and self-doubt that makes you question yourself when you are doing your best.

If I am doing my best, why is my life still challenging?

Your life is the best it can be, given the knowledge, experiences, and solutions available to you at the time. You think your life is not going well because you are judging yourself as not good enough. When you accept responsibility for the life you have, you begin to live your life fully, with truth and honesty.

If you want a better life, ask yourself what you could do to improve your situation. There are many opportunities available, which you may not see because you believe you are not good enough to take advantage of them. To improve your life, you may choose to go to classes to improve your job skills, or you could move to a new location—one that better suits your passions. Realize that given your present situation, you are doing your best. When you move to a different location, or finish your education, you will be doing the best you can with your new knowledge and location. If you continue to improve your life you will always be doing the best you can with this new knowledge.

Doing the best you can is not a putdown or a comment of ridicule. It is an understanding that there is no need for harsh self-criticism when it comes to the choices you have made in your life. It is also accepting who you are with love and compassion, without the need to judge yourself as unworthy of a better life.

Should I accept where I am and leave it at that?

When you accept that you are doing your best, you then stop the almost constant negative conversation you have with yourself about the quality of your life or the decisions you have made. Once this negative conversation ends, you begin to experience your life in a more loving and meaningful way. There is always room for learning and growth in your life. The intention is to do so without negative self-judgement.

How do I move to a healthier place emotionally, if I do not judge or criticize myself?

You can move forward to a more loving and compassionate place emotionally without self-judgement or being critical of your life. As you accept that you are doing your best, you start each day with a fresh, optimistic outlook. Judging yourself is counterproductive to living your best life. If you criticize yourself in an attempt to guide your life to a better place, you add strength to your self-doubt which reinforces your negative self-talk.

Is it possible to accept that you are doing your best, while you work toward what makes you feel better about your life? It can be as simple as asking yourself, "What went well today?" Then changing your focus to what went well, instead of criticizing yourself for what did not go well for you.

Will I grow emotionally if I focus on what is benefiting my life, instead of criticizing myself for not being good enough?

No lasting growth comes from harsh self-judgement or self-criticism. This type of thought pattern only stalls growth and positive learning. When you accept that you are doing your best, you open the door to new possibilities. Yet to accept these opportunities you must be in a loving state of mind.

Imagine your thoughts on a balance scale, one side is filled with regret, criticism, and self-doubt. The other is brimming with joy, truth, honesty, and love. Negativity is heavy and weighs the scale down. Positivity is weightless, airy, and filled with light. When you focus on the positive aspects of your life, you are able to elevate your emotions to ones more beneficial to you throughout your life. This is where you find the emotional growth you are seeking. By releasing your harsh self-judgement, you begin to accept who you are at this moment in time.

Explain, "Who I am at this moment in time."

When you judge yourself, you are rarely in the present moment. If it sounds like this, "I could have done better," or "I should have known better," you are judging yourself for a past experience. Even if it was five minutes ago, you are still judging yourself for your past actions. When you recognize you are doing the best you can, you are accepting who you are in the present moment. You become more accepting of yourself if you say, "I did the best I could, and I am moving forward with the positive lessons I have learned." You allow yourself to experience much more self-love and self-compassion, thereby acknowledging who you are in the present moment.

What is the connection between the present moment and doing my best?

You are in the present moment as you read this, there is no other place you can be. It is impossible to focus on the task at hand while thinking of how you behaved last week. You cannot change your past, no matter how harshly you criticize yourself for not being good enough; although you can adjust how you feel about yourself in this moment. Are you doing your best at this moment? The true and authentic answer is yes. Yet if the answer is no, it is because you are judging yourself against a standard other than truth and self-love.

Accepting that your strength and power are in the present moment, you can move to a healthier place emotionally. In this improved emotional state of mind, you recognize that you are doing the best you can, without the need for self-judgement.

There is nothing you can do about your past. A constant rethinking of past situations will hold you in the past emotionally and prevent you from living in the present moment. It is also important to know that in your past you did the best you could. Even if things did not work out the way you expected, you still did your best.

Is it possible to use, "I'm doing the best I can," as an excuse for not doing much in life?

If you choose to use this as an excuse for not moving forward, your life will be filled with one unsatisfying experience after another. You would feel an inner discomfort that would constantly cause you to question your thoughts and actions. If you use this as an excuse, you may be able to fool those around you for a short while, but you will never be able to fool your authentic self. Connecting with your authentic self is where you realize you do not have to make excuses for your life. Your authentic self is a source of pure love, one that never judges, and is always guiding you to the best life possible.

You cannot fool your authentic self in to thinking you are pursuing your dreams when you are not. Any excuses you use reveal to you the separation between what you are experiencing in life and your inner truth. When you believe you are doing the best you can, you have no need to make excuses for the way your life is unfolding. Excuses or not, you are always doing your best.

At times life is tough, and I feel I'm not doing anything well. Am I doing the best I can in these moments as well?

These are the times to recognize that you are doing your best, so you can release any self-judgement you may be experiencing. In tough times, the last thing you need is to doubt your ability to make the correct decisions or question the courage to move in the right direction. Accepting you are doing your best, gives you the confidence needed in tough times. The moment you accept that you are doing the best you can, you release much of the stress tough times create. Even if you feel you have made a mistake, knowing you have done the best you could—given the knowledge you had at the time—eases the need for harsh self-judgement. Within life's challenges there is tremendous learning if you are open to the possibilities. These experiences cause lasting emotional growth.

I have a need for harsh self-judgement?

Throughout your day, there are times you may judge certain aspects of your life. You judge yourself on how you look, how you solved a problem at work, or even how well you cooked dinner. You may be comparing yourself against an extremely high standard. This judgement does not serve you well, yet you continue to judge yourself anyway.

People believe that by judging themselves they become better, yet they fail to understand that there is no lasting growth found in harsh self-judgement. When you arrive at a better emotional place, you again judge yourself against this unreachable standard.

This can become a never-ending cycle causing increased uncertainty within you. Your need for self-judgement is the false belief that through this behavior you become a better person. Yet you will never be comfortable with who you are if you keep judging yourself for not doing better.

What is wrong with forcing myself to do better?

There will be little lasting growth by forcing yourself to do or learn anything. All people learn and mature easier in a loving and compassionate environment. To better yourself, the healthiest atmosphere is one that surrounds you with love and compassion, not an atmosphere of self-ridicule and self-destructive thoughts. If you want to be better because it excites you, this is wonderful, but if you force yourself to be better there will be some self-resentment.

Constantly judging yourself is not the way to build your self-worth or expand your self-love. To judge yourself is to slowly erode your self-value by using these negative thoughts as a way to measure your worth and self-esteem. Having self-destructive thoughts is behaving in a way you know is not good for you, yet you do so anyway.

How does this relate to the realization that I'm doing the best I can?

When people ignore their inner voice telling them they are doing their best, they are behaving this way for a reason, although this reason may be unknown to them. They may lack an awareness of their self-love. Doing the best you can means accepting that you are worthy of the best possible life your self-love will provide. The way to accomplish this is to silence your self-judgement and ignore the negative opinions of others, and then to accept your own self-love and self-worth. It will not be achieved through critical self-judgement. If you think this negative behavior causes you to grow in loving, compassionate ways, understand it may only bring more uncertainty in to your life.

Is there a way to judge myself without causing discomfort within me?

Judge yourself for all the good and positive things you are doing in your life. If you feel there is little you are doing well, then this is a sign you are not treating yourself kindly. Through the realization you are doing the best you can, you begin to see the favorable aspects of your authentic self, as well as the worthwhile consequences of your actions. Focusing on these positive life experiences changes the way you see yourself and the way the world sees you.

Are the other people in my life doing the best they can as well?

If you believe another person could be doing better than they are, you are judging them based on what you think is right for them and how you imagine their lives should be. There is no way for you to truly know what is going on in the lives of other people. You could guess, but you would be wrong. Once you accept you are doing your best it may be easier to understand that those around you are doing the same as well. Even if their behavior does not please you, they are doing the best they can based on their life experiences and the knowledge they possess at the time. If you are asking them to do better, it is often because you want them to change their behavior to please you.

When it's someone close to you who you judge as not doing enough, the best you could do is ask them what you could do to help them improve their situation. Knowing that everyone is doing their best, you can learn to accept other people for who they are in the present moment.

When you judge other people, you are deeming them unworthy of your love and compassion. Often you are behaving this way to boost your own self-worth, making yourself feel better by putting others down. This will cause you to experience an inner discomfort that is the separation between your inner self-love and your ego.

What happens if I accept that all people are doing their best?

You will begin to experience more satisfying relationships, better job experiences, and even your interactions with people you do not know will go smoothly. The reason for this is because you have released your need to judge others as not being good enough. You now see them for who they are without the cloud of judgement. You also feel relief from not having to tell people how you think they should be living their lives.

By recognizing that all people are doing the best they can, you realize each person is responsible for the outcome of their own lives. Accepting that your life is your responsibility can silence your self-judgement and your judgement of others. You understand that everyone is doing their best no matter how easy or how challenging their life appears.

I understand my life is my responsibility, yet how does this relate with doing the best I can?

If you accept that your life is your responsibility, it becomes easier to see you are doing your best. Your decisions will be based on what you know to be true and right for you. When you are making the right decisions for favorable life experiences, you are doing the best you can. You know your responsibilities toward yourself, and you know how you want your life to turn out. Through this thought process, you are doing your best, based on the information you have at the time. Taking full responsibility for your life is one of the most beneficial things you can do for yourself and those around you.

When life works out well for you, you'll feel wonderful, excited, and pleased you found the courage to make the right choices. This is an indication you are doing well with your personal responsibilities. If events do not work out as you had planned, accept your responsibility for the outcome. Then acknowledge you have done the best you could and learn from the experience.

When things do not work out for me, and I tell myself I could have done better, is there anything else I should do?

In every situation there are variables you cannot control. You may have done the best you could, even though the outcome did not satisfy you. Every experience in life holds within it important lessons for your emotional growth. If the experience did not work out as you had planned, look for the positive lesson, and then use this lesson to gain more skill and knowledge. It does not mean you should have pushed yourself harder. All this means is there were other factors outside of your control. There is little emotional growth when you feel you have not done enough to accomplish the task at hand. If you accept there is always learning in any situation, good or bad, successful or not, you begin to see the positive messages within the outcome.

If I'm doing my best, should I allow the opinions of other people to affect me?

The opinions of other people are based on their life experiences and may not reflect what is true and right for you. When you begin to trust your authentic self, you no longer need the opinions of others to validate your choices. The opinions that matter the most are the ones which are true for you, not the casual opinion of your friends or those you work with. These relationships are important, yet you cannot use the opinions of others as a gauge for your inner happiness. If you firmly believe you are doing the best you can, given the situation, then trust you have done your best.

You may have to seek guidance regarding a project at work. In these situations, the opinions of other people do matter. However, when it comes to your self-worth and your inner happiness, the opinions of others should not be placed in higher regard than the positive opinions you know to be true and right for you.

When I'm unhappy and feeling I could be doing better, the opinions of those around me may help me get back to a better place. What then?

If you are unhappy, a positive opinion can be a boost to your emotional state of mind. Although, if you depend on these opinions as a gauge of your self-worth and self-respect, it will be useful to discover your self-love so you can release your need for their opinions. Learning to trust that you are always doing your best, gives you the strength to fend off your need for the opinions of other people.

As you gain strength in your self-worth you are also discovering your self-love. There is little self-love if you berate yourself for not doing better. While being negative toward yourself, it becomes easy to accept the negative opinions of other people, as well as the self-abuse that happens while in your negative frame of mind.

Why is it people have an opinion that everyone should be doing better?

The people in your life have taught you, you could always be doing better, no matter what the circumstances. The reason for this opinion is because they have been taught the same thing by the people in their lives. Few people know the life experiences others have gone through. It is unrealistic to expect other people to do better if they are doing the best they can. No person should judge another person for not doing enough, because judgement hinders the ability to see the fullness of the person being judged.

If I am a team leader at work, how do I keep people motivated without judging them?

Lead your team with positive reinforcement. Think of how you feel when someone helps you improve at work, as opposed to someone belittling you for making a mistake. It is much more productive to accept that all people are doing the best they can, given what they know at the time. As a team leader it will benefit you to move in a positive direction with this mindset. Because of your positive approach of non-judgement, and supporting your team, you will see more production and better attitudes from those you are trying to lead.

Will I have more compassion and kindness toward other people, if I accept that all people including myself, are doing our best?

This is the intention behind releasing the false belief that everyone could be doing better. There becomes no need to judge or be condescending toward others. You may have no idea what struggles they face in their lives. Only from a place of inner love can you accept with love and compassion that all people, including yourself, are doing their best.

YOUR SELF-DOUBT IS NOT THE TRUE YOU.

Self-Doubt

Is self-doubt a common occurrence in your life? Does self-doubt enter your thoughts when things do not go your way? During the course of your life has self-doubt become a familiar emotion? Do you mistake self-doubt for your inner voice as many people do? Is it possible to release the harmful thought patterns of self-doubt, so you can find the courage to confidently pursue the choices that are true and right for you? What can you do to silence your self-doubt?

People know self-doubt as the voice inside their head preventing them from living a complete life. This powerful negative emotion may hinder their ability to advance to a better job, move to a healthier location, or ask that special person out for tea.

Self-doubt can be so influential it can keep a person from fulfilling their life dreams. With the almost constant messages of negative self-talk floating around in the mind, self-doubt can grow to have tremendous strength. It can be difficult to release self-doubt from your consciousness, because it may have become a large part of your life. How do you move past self-doubt to a place of discovering your self-worth and experiencing your inner self-love?

Throughout your childhood, there were times when you were allowed to explore the world on your own. This was exciting, and also challenging. Some of your expeditions went smoothly, while others may not have worked out as you had planned. Those that turned out poorly, planted the seeds of doubt within you. The interesting thing about self-doubt is once it starts to set roots you never fully release it from your consciousness.

Think back to a time when you attempted to do something new only to see it fail. Ask yourself, do you still maintain this negative opinion of the event? Do you feel the negative emotion of failure when you think of that time? Have you tried this experience again since your initial failure? This is the power of self-doubt. It has stayed with you throughout your life, becoming harder to move past this emotional roadblock. You may never realize the power self-doubt has on altering the course of your life.

What do you have to do to move away from your self-doubt? How can you experience a better self-loving life? Accept that you are doing—and have always been doing—the best you can in any situation. Self-doubt can be created by the false beliefs taught to you during the course of your life. Much of your self-doubt is a lie, built from the negative opinions you believe about yourself and the false beliefs you hold that no longer serve you. Once you recognize the lies in your self-doubt you can begin to move in a direction that is true and right for you.

The person you see reflected in your self-doubt is not the true you. Your authentic self is always loving, supportive and compassionate. There will never be any negative self-talk or self-defeating words spoken by your loving inner voice. You allow your self-doubt to survive by feeding it the negative self-talk you believe as true. Accepting who you are with love and compassion will be the path to silencing your self-doubt and replacing it with the voice of self-love.

Everyone has self-doubt. Why is releasing self-doubt from our consciousness important to living a complete life?

Self-doubt prevents you from experiencing the life you have always wanted to live. It also causes tremendous uncertainty within you, thereby affecting any long-term relationships. When you are unsure which direction to choose because of self-doubt, it has the potential to keep you in an uncomfortable emotional state for years. This subject is important because self-doubt is destructive to you and your life dreams. You may be preventing yourself from moving forward in life because you believe the negative self-talk and self-doubt that keeps repeating in your mind. Realize self-doubt is a roadblock hindering your ability to live a complete life.

How does self-doubt begin in the first place?

Self-doubt originates with the false beliefs you have been taught from an early age. Through negative events and disappointments in life your beliefs grow in strength to become a breeding ground for self-doubt. It does not take much to increase the amount of self-doubt when you have a mindset that doubts your ability to succeed at any task you set out to accomplish. If you believe the negative things about your life more than you trust the positive experiences you have had, these negative beliefs will overshadow your self-confidence. In this frame of mind, self-doubt becomes your natural state of being. You will experience doubt before any other beneficial emotions are felt.

Self-doubt is so powerful it can become my normal baseline belief about myself so I would doubt myself first?

The false beliefs that have become your baseline emotions add strength to your self-doubt. This mindset can create a never-ending cycle of self-doubt. The acceptance of your false beliefs is also the acceptance of your self-doubt. Your doubt then feeds other false beliefs while your self-doubt grows in strength. In contrast, when you release the root of your self-doubt, you also weaken your false beliefs. As a result, your focus will shift away from self-doubt toward the strength and clarity of your inner self-love and self-worth.

People fail to move forward toward their dreams because their self-doubt can be so strong. This behavior adds more strength to their self-doubt, proving their doubt to be true. Some would call this a false positive. Your doubt is a false belief, created from your fear of not moving forward because of your doubt. A thought process such as this, matches what you think is true for you. You might say to yourself, "My doubt was correct, I cannot do this activity, or perform that task at work." Unknown to you is that in false beliefs such as these, you are building a stronger foundation of self-doubt. You are validating your self-doubt by not having the courage to challenge your false beliefs or your doubt.

How do I move past my self-doubt in to a more loving, compassionate state of mind?

There is no love in your self-doubt. This is one way to know if it is true inner guidance or not. When you hear the voice of self-doubt, you can say, "No, this doubt is not true for me." This may sound like an uncommon approach, yet in time you will gain more confidence and comfort challenging your doubt. Your self-doubt is not your inner truth and there is no truth in self-doubt. Your inner truth is one of love and compassion, spoken to you with courage and honesty.

Is self-doubt a lie?

Your authentic self is founded in love and compassion. Self-doubt is neither. Created from a lack of self-confidence, you listen to the lies of self-doubt, and over time you may begin to believe these lies as true. The beliefs at the root of your self-doubt do not move you forward in a loving, compassionate way. Self-doubt is a self-defeating and unloving state of mind.

What are some of the ways I can move away from self-doubt?

One of the ways to move past self-doubt is to accept that you are always guided by your loving inner voice. This voice only speaks its love for you. When you begin to repeat a negative thought or doubt yourself, work to shift your focus away from your doubt to a place of joy and happiness. From here it will be easier to recognize your inner voice.

Another way to move past your self-doubt is to challenge the beliefs at the root of your doubt. Any thought or belief not founded in love is a thought or belief worth challenging and discarding from your consciousness. When you release these thoughts and beliefs, it becomes easier to recognize the love spoken by your inner voice.

Your self-doubt feeds off of any uncertainty you may have about yourself or the choices you make. When you are experiencing self-doubt, there may be a lack of courage needed to fend off this doubt or to silence your self-ridicule. Your inner voice loves you no matter what is happening in your life. As you learn to trust your inner voice, you will always have the loving support needed to make the true and right decisions for the best outcome possible.

Is my inner voice the voice that tells me I could be doing better, or I should be doing better?

This is the voice of negative self-talk feeding your self-doubt. Any voice that speaks nonstop about how you should be doing more with your life without any positive, loving support is a voice worth ignoring. Negative self-talk never speaks its love for you, it only criticizes and causes you to doubt yourself. Loving guidance from your inner voice is always supportive, kind, and compassionate.

Don't I grow emotionally from a little self-doubt every once in a while?

Thinking that growth comes from self-doubt reveals how much doubt is a part of your life. Here is a thought for you, there is no doubt in nature. The mighty redwood tree has no doubt it will grow tall and strong. People will often doubt many aspects of their physical and emotional lives. There is little growth if you allow self-doubt and negative self-talk to direct your life. True positive growth occurs when it is cultivated with love and compassion.

Don't I challenge myself when I experience self-doubt?

You challenge yourself because you allow self-doubt to limit your forward progress. Imagine entering a running race with the doubt you will finish. Guess what? You will never finish with that false belief. You have failed yourself before you even started the race. Furthermore, dropping out of the race will add strength to your self-doubt. You have proven to yourself your doubt was correct. This is how you add strength to your self-doubt.

Now imagine the same foot race with the positive belief you will finish the race. When you do finish the race, you are joyful about your success. If for some reason you do not finish, at least you have given yourself the best chance possible.

Having a positive, loving mindset gives you the opportunity to succeed with any task you set out to accomplish. Starting with a positive outlook is much more beneficial than starting from a belief of self-doubt. You often place the challenge of self-doubt in your own way, but you can remove this obstacle with a positive, self-loving attitude.

Don't people learn and grow from challenges?

People do learn from challenges, but not from those they place in their own way to make the task more difficult to achieve. True learning comes from discovering the positive lessons in challenging situations. Finding the positive lesson in a challenge is a tremendous place for learning and growth that does not involve self-doubt. Any challenge made harder because of self-doubt will be a step backwards when it comes to self-acceptance and understanding.

How will I know I am going in the right direction if I release my self-doubt? There are times self-doubt causes me to stop and reevaluate my course of action. What then?

In this case you are learning that the negative feeling of self-doubt is a sign you are going in the wrong direction. You have the courage to understand the meaning of your doubt and choose a different course of action. If you doubt the road you are traveling is correct, then it is time to stop, look at a map, or ask for directions. This is helpful doubt. Yet if you doubt your ability to accomplish a task, then continue to doubt yourself throughout the project, this is an unhealthy type of doubt.

Positive doubt can be beneficial, but it is still doubt, and it can become stronger as more focus is placed on it. It would be better for you to follow the guidance from your inner voice for the answers you are seeking. The habit of asking for guidance instead of waiting for doubt to overcome you, will benefit you throughout the course of your life. Doubt can quickly build in strength, and before you know what is happening, you might find yourself in an uncomfortable situation.

Is it possible for other people to add strength to my self-doubt?

Self-doubt is an emotional weakness within you. In this weakened emotional state, the opinions of others may have a large impact on how you view yourself. If you give power to their opinions and you lack the strength needed to fend off their negative views, your doubt will deepen to become a place of severe discomfort.

Can I add strength to the self-doubt of those around me?

You can add strength to the self-doubt of those in your life, causing their doubt to gain strength. To prevent this, when you are sharing an opinion, make sure your opinion is founded in love. This will support them on their journey, instead of adding to their challenges.

Your words have tremendous power. These words, if used carelessly, add strength to the self-doubt of another person. Recognize the intention behind the words you speak, because this will make you more mindful if you are saying something loving and positive, or not.

When in a place of self-doubt, the words of others appear to be amplified, sounding louder than they are, and even felt on a more profound level than they normally would. Negative words have a deep impact on those who are struggling emotionally.

Is it possible doubt can become so strong it deepens in to other serious emotional conditions?

Think for a moment of the times you have experienced self-doubt; the strength of this emotion can cause a rough road back to a place of certainty. When self-doubt occurs for a long period of time, and someone adds strength to your doubt through ridicule or condemnation, you begin to undergo unhealthy emotions. Eventually you will experience physical ailments as well. Self-doubt grows in strength from a lack of self-love and self-worth. If you are experiencing self-doubt, it is likely you are also lacking the inner courage needed to silence your doubt. In this negative place, you do not have the confidence you once had, thereby allowing your doubt to cause physical and emotional discomfort in your life.

Self-doubt is that powerful?

Consider the things you doubt in your life: love, trust, your health, your inner voice, or your ability to be or do anything your heart desires. In the emotional state of self-doubt, you even doubt your own self-worth and then make yourself physically sick because of your lack of inner trust. Self-doubt is a powerful negative emotion few people realize can cause tremendous stress and anxiety within them. Self-doubt also causes you to be afraid of doing anything that would improve your life for fear of being wrong or failing.

The reason for discussing self-doubt, is to guide you to an emotional place that is healthier for you, a place where there is only love and compassion. This is where you will discover your inner voice and the self-love that has always been within you. Self-doubt has the power to deny you of your self-love, as well as other positive emotions that are beneficial for you.

If I am deep in self-doubt what are some of the ways I can move to a better emotional state of mind?

To move away from deep self-doubt, look within yourself to discover the infinite abundance of love always flowing to you and through you. The source of this love is your authentic self who has nothing but love, kindness, and compassion for you. Know that by accepting your self-doubt you are believing a lie that has no foundation in love or truth. When you are deep in doubt, you are preventing this flow of love from lifting you to a healthier emotional state of mind.

It can be a gradual journey back to experiencing your inner love, but the journey starts the moment you choose to focus on things that bring joy and happiness in to your life. Changing your focus to more positive thoughts will help you get started. Before too long you will have shifted your attention away from your self-doubt to a place more honest and loving.

Any other advice?

This is a journey to a more positive, self-loving, experience. The recommendation is to work toward what makes you feel better about yourself, without having to relive the reasons for your doubt. Also, strive to appreciate the positive aspects of your life. This helps you shift your focus to one that is more loving and compassionate.

Appreciating myself when I am experiencing self-doubt seems odd?

This is not an ego-driven act of appreciation. This is a kind, gentle, loving act of gratitude intended to lift your emotional state of mind in a positive direction. Appreciating yourself is as simple as appreciating what sets you apart from the people in your life. Any skill, any talent, anything positive about yourself is worth appreciating. This will help you change your focus from the negative feeling of self-doubt to a more positive feeling of self-love.

You may also take a walk in the park and appreciate the warmth of the sun or the flowers you see. Simply find positive things to help change your focus. As you continue to concentrate on appreciating the world around you, you begin to move in to a more self-loving state of mind.

It seems it takes tremendous strength and courage to overcome self-doubt and replace it with appreciation?

The inner strength needed to overcome any obstacle in your life is rooted in self-love. If the intention is to lift yourself out of self-doubt and away from negative thoughts, you have the strength of your inner love to do so. Once you become comfortable with appreciating life, you move in to a more self-loving, compassionate state of mind. If your desire is to release yourself from self-doubt, you will find more than enough strength and courage to accomplish your task.

It must be my self-doubt telling me I have never felt this inner love or strength.

It can be no voice other than the voice of self-doubt. True loving guidance is only spoken by your authentic self. You may confuse your loving inner voice with the other voices that constantly speak negative words and reinforce negative thoughts. Self-doubt may try to convince you that you do not have a loving inner voice.

I have heard from others I should ignore all the voices I hear in my mind. How do I resolve this?

Many people have not taken the necessary time to explore and discover their loving inner voice. They believe this loving voice does not exist because it may be overshadowed by their self-doubt and negative self-talk. The voice to listen for and acknowledge is the only voice that is loving and compassionate toward you, and those in your life. Your loving inner voice never advises you to harm anyone by your words or actions. This authentic voice will only speak to you with love, kindness, and compassion.

Some people believe in a "tough love" attitude when it comes to a person who is experiencing negative emotions. How would this fit in with a conversation about self-doubt?

Tough love may work well in some cases, yet this type of attitude can cause great harm when it comes to someone who is in a state of deep self-doubt. Speaking harshly to someone who is in need of a kind word will not suddenly make their self-doubt go away. It may satisfy the speaker, yet it will not make the person who is experiencing self-doubt feel any better.

If the intention is to express love and help the person move through their self-doubt, then there is no reason for this form of behavior. People feel the intention behind the words they hear whether it is positive or negative. It is the emotion of the intention that indicates if the words are spoken from a place of loving truth or not.

If I am trying to talk myself out of self-doubt, is it possible to feel the truth behind the words I'm saying to myself?

When you speak words of self-love and compassion you feel the truth in these words. Even if you do not believe these words, the intention will have a positive impact on your healing. Speaking positive, loving words is one way to move away from the negativity of self-doubt. You can also silence your negative self-talk with positive words. This keeps you from slipping in to self-doubt when you first notice the beginning of the negative emotion.

There seems to be a lot of fear in self-doubt?

Fear will be found in situations where people doubt themselves when it comes to the decisions they must make for a better life. In times of uncertainty and self-doubt, a person will experience an element of fear. The question arises, "What if I make the wrong choices, what then?" There is both fear and self-doubt in this question as these emotions support and give strength to each other. Through a constant exposure to self-doubt a person has the potential to experience a debilitating level of fear. Being unsure of what to do or say will cause both doubt as well as an inner fear, preventing a person from taking positive action.

What am I afraid of when I experience self-doubt?

Your main fear may be, "What if my self-doubt is correct?" This question adds strength to your fear, as well as to your self-doubt. What could be harder to accept? Your doubt or the fear of proving your doubts? Either way, these emotional questions cause tremendous uncertainty within you. When you work to release your self-doubt, you also release the fear of moving toward a healthier life.

You may also experience other fears associated with self-doubt, trying something you have never done before, may be one. Others could be the fear of failure, looking like a novice, or the fear of success, which may also add strength to your self-doubt.

My self-doubt can create a fear that could prove my doubts to be true?

Imagine someone close to you adding strength to your self-doubt. If this is constant, your fear builds. In time, you begin to think they may be right in their evaluation of you. What do you do? You know who you are, yet they keep adding strength to your self-doubt. Then your fear builds. You may ask yourself, "What if they are right?" This increases your self-doubt; at the same time your fear grows in strength as well. This is how you find yourself in a deep place of self-doubt because you have begun to believe your doubt, and this makes you fearful your doubt is true.

Is there an end to this cycle?

The way to stop this cycle of self-doubt is to accept that for your own happiness no other opinion about yourself matters, except your own loving one. Finding your loving inner voice among the voices of self-doubt and negative self-talk will be the guiding light you have been seeking throughout this self-destructive cycle. Your inner voice is always supportive, never judgmental. It is always loving and compassionate. This is the voice of who you are at all times, speaking to you through love and compassion. Any other voice you hear is not your authentic truth. To stop the cycle of self-doubt and fear, discover and accept the love from your inner voice, then live life with this love as your foundation.

ONLY YOU KNOW WHAT IS TRUE AND RIGHT FOR YOU.

The Opinions of Other People

Opinions can be a welcome source of guidance when you are working on a project with others, choosing a contractor to paint your house, or finding a car suitable to your needs. People often look to others for advice when they doubt themselves or feel uncertain which direction is best. The opinions of a trusted friend may be beneficial, but these opinions can alter the course of your life.

Opinions can also add tremendous confusion and uncertainty to a situation. Why do you place so much trust in the beliefs of others when it comes to important aspects of your life? Their opinions may be appropriate for their lives, but they may not be relevant to yours. Do their opinions bring you a level of comfort, even though they may prevent you from trusting yourself?

Often, opinions are based on what other people have experienced in their lives and what they believe is right for them. Your opinions are created the same way. They are based on your life experiences. Even though your opinions may have value to you they may not align with the values of others.

When it comes to sharing your opinion with people you may not have a complete understanding of what they have gone through in their lives. Your opinion may have merit yet there is always a bit of bias in any opinion. This bias may confuse those who are seeking guidance because your opinion may not resonate with their truth. This is why following the opinions of others without question can lead someone in the wrong direction.

From a young age you have been taught to seek the opinions of teachers, family members, and close friends, on every subject imaginable. You may have been taught that those around you may have a better idea of what is right for you. As time passes, your trust in their opinions grows, causing you to seek outside advice before you look within yourself for guidance. You learned to trust these opinions over what you felt or what you knew to be true for you. In a subtle way you have given your decision-making responsibilities to those who will gladly offer their opinion. Through this process you have learned to doubt and second-guess yourself when it comes to making the right choices for your life. The inner guidance you are intended to learn and trust has been overshadowed by the desire to seek advice from other people.

Through this process, you have become disconnected from your loving inner voice that is constantly directing you to the exact answers and guidance you are seeking. If you feel any uncertainty about the opinions of other people, it is this feeling that is the difference between their opinions, and what is true and right for you.

People often confuse their negative self-talk with their inner voice. When you accept your negative self-talk as true, there is little trust in yourself. This is why you look for the opinions of others to make it through your day. Your inner voice is the voice of your intuition and instincts. These feelings have your best interests as their main focus. There is no reason for your inner voice to give you misleading advice or lead you astray when asking for guidance. This powerful voice will always advise you through love and compassion. As you learn to trust yourself, your need for the opinions of others will fade.

My inner voice and the opinions of other people, what is the connection?

Your inner voice may have been overshadowed by the opinions of those around you. You trust their advice over what your inner voice knows to be best for you. Throughout this process you have built a strong trust in the guidance of other people. You believe they know better than you about the important questions you are asking. As you learn to focus on your inner voice and its loving guidance, you will discover you need fewer opinions to make it through your day.

What is wrong with the opinions of those around me?

There is nothing wrong with the opinions of others, although their opinions may not be correct for your present situation. Their opinions are based on what is right for them, yet they may contradict the inner guidance you receive from your intuition and instincts. There are people you trust and those whose wisdom you admire, however, their guidance may not be as thorough as the advice you receive from your inner voice.

Is it a problem if the opinions of other people help me move forward with a life task?

When you ask for an opinion or advice, it is because you do not trust yourself to find the answer within you. The opinions of others may be beneficial to you from time to time, yet in the long run your inner voice will guide you to what is right for you at all times. As you learn to trust your inner voice, you begin to make healthier choices that are more favorable for you than if you had asked someone their opinion.

Before I ask for an opinion, I could ask myself what should I do? I did ask, and that is why I'm asking for an opinion.

Learning to trust yourself when it comes to the choices in life might be frightening and challenging. Your true inner voice knows the answers to your questions. Yet, you may not have cultivated the level of trust needed to follow through with the guidance you receive. You may have to sift through your negative self-talk and self-doubt in order to hear your loving inner voice. When you take the time to hear and then trust your inner voice, you become more confident in the decisions you have to make in every aspect of your life.

I should learn to trust my inner voice and then I'll not need the opinions of other people to make it through my day?

Learning to trust your inner voice will be to your advantage throughout your life. No person truly knows what is going on in your life, and because of this their opinion may not be well suited to your situation. Although the opinion of someone you trust may be beneficial, know when to follow your inner voice and when to ask for advice from others.

How will I know which is right for me, the guidance from my inner voice or the advice of a trusted friend?

Your inner voice speaks through your intuition and gut feelings. These sources of guidance always have your best interests as their main priority. When you pay attention to these feelings you will know the right course of action to take. This offers you the best way to know what is true and right for you. As you learn to trust your inner voice, you gain the confidence needed to live life without relying on the opinions of other people.

The opinions of a close and trusted friend can help you sort through the options regarding any decision. You can use these opinions as a comparison to feel your way to what is right for you. There is no harm in asking for advice from a close friend though it is important to also become aware of the truth your inner voice speaks to you through your emotions and intuition.

Recently a friend spoke a hurtful, negative opinion of me. How am I to handle this?

Your friend may be trying to make themselves feel better by expressing their negative opinion of you. This is painful. Remember though, an opinion is based on the speaker's point of view, and it may be based on inaccurate information as well. Only you know what is true and right for you. As you come to know the love of your authentic self, you will have the strength and courage to deflect any negative comment or opinion that is not true or is hurtful.

It is surprising a person would speak a hurtful opinion to make themselves feel better. What can we do about this kind of negative behavior?

When you or someone behaves this way, you do so to make yourself feel better. This behavior reveals a low opinion about oneself. Speaking this way is intended to boost one's self-esteem. The intention of discovering your authentic self is to arrive at a stable, emotional state of mind where you are immune from these negative opinions, along with releasing the desire to speak negative opinions of others. It is important to find your inner truth, a place where you are loving and compassionate, where you do not need to express a negative opinion.

Why are negative opinions as powerful as they are?

Opinions are powerful because at one time you may have trusted the person who shared their opinion. When people believe an opinion, strength is added to the opinion. An opinion influences your life because of the amount of energy you focus on it. If someone says something you know to be untrue, you can disregard this opinion without much thought. This will release any negative energy that would have added strength to this opinion.

It can be the same way when a person gives an opinion that is not true or right for you. As you focus on what they have said, you continue to add energy to the comment. Being in a strong place emotionally gives you the opportunity to quickly ignore the comment without much thought or concern. The challenge comes when you are in a vulnerable state of mind. Then the opinion can rapidly feed your insecurities. The longer you focus on it, the more uncertainty it creates within you.

What is the best way to protect myself from the hurt caused by the negative opinions of other people?

Opinions can have the intention of being hurtful, even though the opinions may be untrue. As you become more comfortable hearing your inner voice, you learn of the tremendous love within you. You realize there is an endless flow of this love. You also realize this flow of love is restricted by negativity, self-doubt, and false beliefs. When you learn to access this inner love, you become strong enough to fend off the negative opinions of anyone you encounter in your day.

What about the negative opinions I have about myself? Because of them I surely do not feel any self-love.

This thought pattern has been created by the attention you give to your negative self-talk. An opinion gains strength from your constant focus on the opinion, no matter if it is positive or not. Your authentic self knows these negative self-opinions are untrue. Yet you believe them to be true because you choose to focus on the negatives of life instead of refocusing on the positive aspects of who you are. To release your negative self-opinion, ask yourself, why you continue to add energy to something you know is false or causes you to doubt yourself? The answer will come from your inner voice, speaking its love for you no matter what opinion you have of yourself. You can also block the flow of self-love because of the opinion that an inner voice does not exist, thereby adding strength to this false belief as well.

Living an authentic life is about learning to trust yourself in all aspects of your life. This trust is built on knowing what is true for you, connecting with the eternal love available to you, and then living by this love. As you release the negative opinions of other people and those you have about yourself, you become aware of your true self.

What about seeking an opinion to boost my self-worth?

When you are feeling emotionally low, the kind words of someone can raise your spirits. Sharing words of kindness and compassion are a wonderful way to help someone who is in a negative frame of mind. Seeking an opinion as a way to boost your self-worth is when the opinion causes an issue in your life. In this case you are more concerned with what other people think of you, using their opinion as a way to elevate your self-esteem and strengthen your ego. If you base your self-worth and happiness on the opinions of other people you will find it a difficult need to maintain. You will never be able to support any long-lasting emotional benefit from this type of behavior. As you seek the opinions of others to maintain your value, you continue to diminish your self-worth and self-love.

When you behave this way there will be an underlying feeling of self-rejection. You are refusing to look within and discover your authentic self and the love it has for you. In this case you fear your negative self-talk may be true. The positive opinion of someone close may raise your emotional state of mind, yet if you are creating a life based on their opinions, you are not living your inner truth.

It is considered self-rejection to believe and live by the opinions of others?

If you need the opinions of others to establish your self-worth, you are rejecting your own self-love. Every person you meet will have a different opinion of who they think you are. If you change who you are to satisfy their opinions of who they think you should be, in a short amount of time you will no longer recognize your authentic self. This separates you from knowing the truth of who you are and the love found deep within you. In doing so, you place more value on their opinion of who you are, than on your own opinion of your authentic self.

Why do we continually seek the opinions of other people for our self-worth?

You do so because you do not have a strong connection with your inner truth and your self-love. Another reason may be because you experience an elevated sense of self-worth from the emotional boost these opinions give you. This then becomes an intense need, to maintain this level of elevated self-worth though it is not based on a foundation of true self-love.

That is a powerful need.

Through the opinions of other people, you may see yourself in a more positive way than what you actually believe about yourself. Even though living by the opinions of other people is not experiencing your authentic self, it might be more positive than the opinion you may have toward yourself. To maintain the feeling of self-worth, even though it is not true self-worth, you keep seeking the opinions of others to feel complete.

How do opinions about me differ from my true self?

When you were growing up, you trusted the people around you and believed they spoke the truth. Yet not everything they said was true for you. It may have sounded something like this, "You are tone deaf, you will never sing well," or "You are not smart enough to understand higher mathematics." Comments such as these started as opinions. As time went on, you may have begun to believe these opinions as true. Through these false beliefs, you created an opinion of yourself that you could not sing, or you have difficulty understanding math. These opinions may not represent your true self. They were based on what others believed to be true about you.

You trusted the people who spoke these opinions, you convinced yourself these false beliefs were true, without trying to prove them wrong. You may sing perfectly well, but you are too afraid to try because of a false belief that started as an opinion—an opinion you held onto throughout your life and may still believe. During this time your inner voice was speaking its love to you and giving you reasons to trust yourself. Yet you chose not to listen because you learned to trust the opinions of other people, more than you trusted your true self.

Why is it I trust the opinions of others, more than what I think is best for me?

You have taught yourself that the opinions of other people are better suited for your life than what you know to be best for you.

You often forget you know more about what you need for a fulfilling life than any other person. A trusted friend may help you with their guidance, but as you learn to trust yourself, you will know what is true and right for you at all times.

How do I overcome the challenges of learning to trust myself enough, so I do not have to seek opinions as a way to live my life?

Learn to trust your loving, caring, inner voice that is always guiding you to what is right for you through every decision. As you gain trust in the guidance you receive from your inner voice, your self-confidence will build in strength. This trust allows you to experience your self-love and your self-worth on a more truthful level than ever before.

Do our opinions of other people interfere with the way our relationships unfold?

An opinion can cloud your ability to see people clearly. If you always see your opinion instead of seeing the truth of a person, you deny yourself the benefits of being true to yourself, as well as failing to recognize the truth of who they are. This behavior limits the potential of your relationship. In doing so you block your ability to truly know this person because you are too focused on your opinion of them. Opinions have the ability to make you blind to the truth of a person.

Is there any judgement in holding an opinion of someone?

There is tremendous judgement within an opinion you hold of someone or yourself. You may have based your opinion on what you have seen or even what you have learned from someone else. In both of these cases there is judgement in the opinion. Think for a moment of a person who appears to be homeless. What comes to mind? What opinion have you formed based on what little you know? Whatever your opinion, you may have judged them unfairly. Your judgement of others prevents you from being kind and compassionate.

I met someone through a friend. Beforehand, this friend expressed an opinion of this person. How should I handle my friend's opinion toward this new person?

The opinion of your friend may not be based on complete facts, or their opinion may have a bias created from their life experiences. If a friend shares an opinion of someone you have yet to meet, this opinion could distort your experience.

Each person may have a different opinion than you on various subjects. This is why trusting the opinions of others can be challenging. You may never know the reason for your friend's opinion. It is best to focus on your encounter with this person, and create an opinion based on the truth of what you have experienced.

What about people who have an exaggerated opinion of themselves?

People who have an exaggerated opinion of themselves do so to boost their self-worth. With people who behave this way, there can be a lack of self-love and self-compassion. They speak highly of themselves as a means to make themselves feel better. This will bring brief comfort, because they do not have a solid foundation of self-love, thereby perpetuating the need to boost their self-esteem through expressing a high self-opinion. They act this way because they assume if they speak highly about themselves then others will begin to think highly of them as well.

Is it possible to add strength to a person's high self-opinion by what I say to them?

If your desire is to be liked by this person, your opinion adds strength to their high self-opinion thus boosting their self-worth. In doing so they may reward you with a higher opinion of you. Yet with this behavior, there can be little truth because each person is changing to fit in to the opinions expressed. You can also boost the opinion of someone as a way to achieve something you desire from them.

How do we use an opinion as a way to achieve something from others?

Often if a person is struggling emotionally, they may not have a positive opinion of themselves. Because of these challenges, their self-worth and trust in themselves may be low. In an attempt to be accepted or find stable footing they may believe an opinion spoken by those around them. It is possible to build up their self-worth by expressing false opinions, thereby controlling them by these opinions. If these opinions continue, they will be drawn to the kind words, even though the intention is to get them to do certain tasks. They are then manipulated by these uplifting opinions, and their need to be liked, loved, or accepted by others.

My opinion of myself could be so low I would be willing to do things for other people, in order for them to have a positive opinion of me?

When you have a low opinion of yourself, it is because you have become separated from your own source of self-love. To elevate your self-worth, you may do things for others, so you receive their positive, supportive opinions. In behaving this way, you have attached your happiness, your self-love and self-worth, to their opinions. If your behavior continues this way you are willingly placing your emotional happiness in the hands of others. You allow them to control you by their opinions.

When you are living a complete life, you do not allow another person to control you emotionally. Also, a person who is in touch with their self-love has no reason to control someone emotionally by manipulating them with an opinion.

There were times in my life when I sought a positive opinion about myself to feel accepted or loved by another person. It's hard to accept that occasionally we look to others for an emotional boost.

Everyone needs an emotional boost once in a while. The problems arise when you seek these opinions as a way to maintain a constant stream of acceptance. If others speak highly of you your self-worth soars, and you feel good about yourself. On the other hand, if they speak harshly of you your self-worth tumbles, and you may fall in to deep self-doubt. When your desire is to be liked by other people as a way to validate your self-worth, you are allowing your emotional happiness to be affected by their opinions.

It is in this emotional state when you are vulnerable to the words and actions of others. Their opinions will never lead you to the unconditional love and happiness you desire. In doing so you have made someone else responsible for your happiness. This is a responsibility they do not want, because they may be working on finding their own inner love and happiness. Your happiness is your responsibility, no matter what other people say about you or how they act toward you.

Your inner self-love is a constant source of love, it does not diminish when your life becomes challenging. This love gives you the strength and courage to handle any struggle you may face. No opinion of you has the same level of love and compassion as the loving opinion of your authentic self.

Should I disregard the opinions that come my way throughout the course of a day?

There are times when an opinion can benefit you. By asking yourself how these opinions make you feel, you will know which opinions to follow and which to discard. A positive opinion from your manager about a project at work can be a boost to the project and alter your standing with your manager.

The intention is to guide you to a place where you can feel the difference between an opinion needing your attention or an opinion you can quickly disregard. Your day will flow smoother when you learn to trust the guidance from your loving inner voice. The need for the opinions of others will fade as you begin to feel and trust your true self-love. You will not need to seek the opinions of other people to boost your self-esteem, because you have learned that your self-love and self-worth will be found within your authentic self.

WHERE YOU CONNECT WITH THE TRUTH AND HONESTY OF WHO YOU ARE.

The Present Moment

You are here in the present moment reading this. Physically, there is no other place you can be but in the here and now. Emotionally, you can be anywhere but in the present moment. Why is it so challenging to be in the here and now emotionally? The present moment is where the action is, not in the past or future. That's because the past and the future do not exist; one is a memory, the other a dream. All you have and all you desire will be found in the present moment.

When you were a child, you lived in the present moment. You wanted to do it now, see it now, and experience it now, you never wanted to wait. Your life was focused in the here and now. The joy and thrill of life was found in the present moment. Is it still this way today? Has time changed your focus, away from the present to the responsibilities of the future? Have you had a life experience that made you avoid being in the present moment emotionally?

There may have been times in your life when the present moment was too painful to endure. You may have retreated to a past memory you knew would give you a better feeling than what you were experiencing at the time. This could have been your way of gaining some control over your life. For those who have experienced past emotional pain, they may have remained in that place since the pain occurred. This is one of the many reasons people keep themselves from experiencing their inner strength and true self-love, found in the present moment. They fear moving forward may be too painful.

If you were to accept that you have been and are always doing the best you can, it may be possible to forgive yourself for carrying the emotional burden of a past pain. Forgiveness helps change your focus so you can then begin to experience life in the present moment. Through the loving act of self-forgiveness, you realize you have the ability to control the outcome of your life. The strength to forgive and move on can only be found in the here and now. The question is, can you forgive yourself and then move in to the present moment? Do you have the courage to leave the past behind and live in the here and now?

Focusing on your past can be enjoyable. For example, telling memorable stories or remembering a positive life changing event. Yet the constant reliving of the past can keep you from experiencing the growth meant for you in the present moment. Focus is an important factor while seeking your inner strength and self-love. Your constant attention on your past can keep you from understanding the lessons your past has to teach you.

Is it possible your current life situation is too challenging to accept the present moment? If so, then focusing on your past may bring a bit of relief, although temporarily. At some point, it becomes beneficial for your well-being to step in to the present moment.

Any negative emotion from your past can be an anchor keeping you from living a complete life. You may be unsure why you were hurt and uncertain how to move forward from this place. This uncertainty may keep you from experiencing the inner strength you need to move away from the past and in to the healing energy of the here and now.

Physically there is nothing you can do about the events of your past, though these memories can continue to be a part of your awareness. However, if you develop the ability to trust the truth of your self-love you can release the hold your past has on you.

The present moment is where you are the most connected to your authentic self. It is in the here and now where you choose to focus on the love and wisdom of your inner voice. With this renewed strength and awareness, you can release your past and then live fully in the present moment. This gives you the courage to live the life you have always wanted to live.

Why is the present moment so powerful?

The present moment is where you connect with the truth and honesty of who you are. Your past is gone, there is nothing you can physically do about it. Yet, with the strength and courage available to you in the present moment, you can turn your perspective within and discover the eternal love within you. This inner love will help you understand that you are doing your best now and while in your past you were doing your best as well. This love gives you the awareness to shift your focus away from the past and recognize the possibilities available when you face life as it is. The emotional strength to overcome any difficulties in your life today or to overcome any emotional struggles leftover from your past will be found within you in the present moment.

My life seems just fine the way it is. Why do I need to focus so intently on the present moment?

Your past has the potential to hold you back from living the life you have always wanted to live. It is possible you may be second-guessing yourself as you allow the past to dictate the outcome of your current life. This may cause you to doubt yourself based on what has happened in your past, thereby limiting how your life expands today. People fail to realize how the impact of a negative experience is carried within them throughout their life, thereby affecting them physically and emotionally.

How does focusing on my past hold me back in the life I am living now?

When your focus is on the past, whether you are focused on a wonderful event or a negative experience, you reignite the emotions of that time. This places you emotionally in your past, possibly denying yourself the self-love available to you right now. For example, telling a funny story from your past triggers the same happy emotions as when you first experienced the funny event. It is the same way with negative experiences. When you think of the reason for your pain, the emotions you felt in your past are experienced in the present moment. These negative emotions may have an influence on how you make decisions now.

How do I resolve the issues that have occurred in my past?

In the here and now, you have the courage to forgive yourself for carrying the burden of a past pain. You then may release the need you have to focus on your past suffering. This allows you to resolve your emotional issues. Through your self-love and inner strength found in the present moment, you can discover the loving place of forgiveness and self-forgiveness. Through the act of forgiveness, you are moving away from your past. Once you are in the present moment you can change the way you experience your past emotionally.

How do I change the way I experience my past by being in the present moment?

You can accept that in your past you did the best you could under the circumstances. Also forgive yourself for the false belief that you could have done better. The power of forgiveness should never be underestimated when the desire is to release the uncomfortable hold a painful past may have on you. By changing your focus away from your negative thoughts about the past toward more positive thoughts, your emotional experience with the past will change. If you constantly focus on a past negative event, you are adding energy and strength to the experience. In doing so, you remain emotionally connected to the event. This prevents you from moving ahead with a clear state of mind.

Why do some people talk about their distant past as if it were just the other day?

For some people, their current life experience may be too challenging for them to accept so their stories bring them a level of comfort. It is possible their present-day concerns are not being heard, so they feel they must speak of the past as a way to experience some level of validation. In a way, they are judging themselves as unworthy of being valued, or recognized by others. This behavior originates from a lack of self-esteem and self-respect.

Others may be stuck in the past emotionally and use their stories as a way to appear relevant. Even though their stories are of the past, they may be experiencing their pain now. They have yet to forgive themselves and move forward in to the present moment. When a person speaks of their past this way, the emotional attachment surrounding their experiences may make it easier for them to go about their day.

The act of forgiveness can move us away from a painful past?

If it is a heartfelt act of forgiveness, an act you believe is the right thing to do, then it will be a loving act meant to release you from a negative history. This act of forgiveness is founded on your desire to be in a more centered place emotionally. Authentic forgiveness can only occur in the here and now. This is where you have the clarity to recognize that holding onto your anger or reliving an emotional trauma does not serve your best interests.

What other factors should we consider if we want to be in the present moment?

In the midst of their busy lives, people fail to recognize the importance of being in the present moment with family and loved ones. This can create a challenge particularly for children as they seek comfort from their parents, only to be pushed away by a phone call or an email that could be answered at a later time. The parent may believe there will always be another time for a loving conversation with a spouse, child, or family member. By becoming conscious of the power in the present moment they will realize that now is the time for these conversations. These moments are not to be put off for another time.

If all we have is the present moment, should we speak honestly with those we love?

Being in the present moment emotionally allows you to realize there is no tomorrow, only now. It is in this place of now where you have the courage to say the loving words needed to be said. If the intention is to resolve an issue with someone, find your inner self-love before you say a word. This will keep you focused because this is where you are the most centered and positive. As you have seen throughout history, lives can change in an instant. There is no need to wait to tell someone how much you care for them. The best time for this conversation is now.

What if my relationship is not going well? How does being in the present moment help me?

Your happiness is your main priority. If your relationship is not going well, there is no point in looking to the past to see who is to blame. With your emotional strength, found in the present moment, you can seek the help you need to continue the relationship or find the courage to search for a better life. You will have more clarity to make the right choices for the best course of action, than you would if you were looking over your past to see what falsehoods have been spoken. You cannot solve a problem today while focused on the past.

The strength to deal with a failing relationship or other stressful situations will be found in the present moment?

In this state of awareness, you now see the path to a resolution clearly, without the emotionally distorted thinking the past generates. When a relationship fails there may be a need to find someone at fault. This is looking in the past for the cause of the failure. It does not matter who is at fault, because your relationship is in trouble. In the present moment you are the strongest and most loving. From this place you can focus on the task at hand without the negative influence of your past.

When you first learned to ride a bicycle, your complete focus was on staying balanced so you would not fall. You were in the present moment. There are times in your life when your focus is strong, similar to learning to ride a bicycle, in situations like these, you are in the here and now.

Countless artists, musicians, and performers—to name a few—are in the present moment as they practice their skill or craft. This is where you are the most connected to your intuition and your inner voice. In this focused frame of mind, you will hear or feel the guidance needed to work through any stressful life challenge. Yet you often choose when to be focused and when other things are more important than being centered in the present moment.

Are there times in life when it is good not to be in the present moment?

If this is the case, be kind to yourself. This could be the result of experiencing powerful emotional or physical pain. As a way to protect yourself from the pain, your mind will take you back to a time in your life when you may have been happier or more comfortable. Try to remain focused in the present moment. It is here where you are better equipped to handle any situation, even a situation that appears to be negative.

In a negative situation it's best to be in the present moment?

In the here and now, you find the clarity unknown to you if your focus is somewhere else emotionally. It is this awareness that gives you the strength and courage to make it through an uncomfortable situation. It is also this clarity which helps you turn a negative situation in to a positive learning experience.

Why is there such clarity in the present moment?

This is where you are in tune with your authentic self. You are also keenly aware of what is happening around you, emotionally and physically. In this heightened state of awareness, you are open to receiving the wisdom of your inner guidance. When you are focused on the past, or too focused on the future, your awareness of the possibilities which will help you is not as strong as it would be if your attention were on the here and now. It is through the clarity in the present moment where you recognize the guidance needed to make the best choices on a more immediate and powerful level.

If I'm too focused on the future, it could hinder my life experience now?

Focusing on the future is more beneficial than focusing on your past, although you can be too focused on either. Any time you are not focused on the present moment, you are taking energy away from the clarity of your authentic self. This clarity allows you to make the best choices based on how the thought of these choices makes you feel.

As with anything taking your thoughts away from the present moment, focusing on the future can become a distraction. If the majority of your thoughts are focused on the future, you have separated yourself from the wisdom available in the present moment. Your strength and ability to guide your life toward the best future will be found in the here and now.

The decisions I make now affect my future, yet how does this help me in the present moment?

At some point your present moment becomes your future, and your future becomes your present moment. People often think of their future, as a time far away—next week, next year, or in ten years. Your future also includes the next thirty minutes. Many of the decisions you make in the present moment affect your immediate future. When you are focused in the here and now the clarity of these decisions is more in line with your true self. You are tapping in to the wisdom of your inner guidance and then using this wisdom to make better choices. If you make choices based on what you think may happen in the future without connecting to this wisdom you are not in the present moment. Why? Because you are not in sync with this inner clarity.

How do I make decisions for my future if I do not focus on how things will turn out?

In the clarity of the present moment, you experience the guidance needed to make these decisions, even if these questions affect your future. You cannot receive guidance if your focus is entirely on the future; there are too many variables affecting the outcome. The advice is to focus on your inner guidance and ask yourself about your future. Then listen to the guidance and react accordingly. This is all you can do, because there is no way for you to predict what may happen in the future. The best thing to do is to follow the inner guidance you receive while in the clarity of the present moment.

It seems counterintuitive to focus on the present moment as a way to find the guidance needed to help me in the future?

Through aligning with the wisdom available in the present moment, you are able to focus on a current or future situation and receive the guidance that will be right for you now. This guidance comes in many forms, yet you will feel the loving answers through your emotions, intuition, and gut feelings. Even if the question is about something in your future, these powerful sources of guidance will lead you in the right direction, all while being in the present moment.

Why is the present moment so powerful?

It is in the present moment where your mind is free from the distractions of the past or the future. This allows you to connect with your true self and your loving inner guidance. In this powerful state of awareness, your physical being, your emotions, your inner guidance, and your authentic self are all in sync with each other. Thereby offering trusted guidance while focusing on the present moment. This is where life takes on a better feeling because you are emotionally centered and rooted in your authentic truth.

Is it possible to fool myself in to thinking I am in the here and now emotionally?

Why try to fool yourself in to thinking you are experiencing the wisdom and guidance found in the present moment? You may think you can fool yourself, but you will never fool your authentic self. This type of behavior would only cause uncertainty in your life. You will feel this is not your truth, and in this false place, you will not be as successful as you would if you were living your truth. The present moment is where you are the most connected to a stream of awareness not available to you when you are focused on the past or the future.

I have met people who will say they are living in the present moment, yet it does not feel genuine. Why do they behave this way?

There are numerous things going on in a person's life you may know nothing about, although you may be able to feel their uncertainty. Oftentimes, there are emotional or physical burdens preventing a person from living in the present moment. They may not want to be in the here and now because they could be experiencing too much physical or emotional pain. In this case, focusing on their past or the distant future is an emotional relief for them. Asking them to be completely in the present moment could be asking them to accept a life they are unwilling or not emotionally strong enough to accept. If they are unable to face their present situation they may retreat to the past as a way to make themselves more comfortable.

Is there any way to help people who experience life this way?

The best you can do for those experiencing emotional or physical challenges is to be loving, kind, and non-judgmental toward them or their circumstances. In every life situation there are lessons to learn. Their lesson may be to discover the love found in their true selves. This gives them the strength and courage to accept that they are doing their best and the love they seek will be found in the present moment.

This brings us back to the people who are stuck in their past because they are unable to accept their present moment experience.

There are reasons why people have yet to discover their self-love and inner strength found in the present moment. They may not have the courage to forgive those who hurt them, nor have they forgiven themselves for what they believe are their life mistakes. Being in the present moment means to accept that if you are unable to change your life you have the courage to change the way you react to life. Through the simple, powerful act of self-forgiveness you achieve the inner strength needed to help you move away from the past and lead you in to the here and now. Your courage and self-love to forgive yourself or forgive other people, are waiting for you in the present moment.

Why is it I cannot forgive myself or others from any place other than the present moment?

As you contemplate the act of forgiveness, your desire is to release the past from controlling your life and then move in to the present moment. You want to forgive without the burden of negative self-judgement, or self-doubt. Forgive yourself for the shame you feel when you think of the people who caused your emotional or physical pain. Your true strength to forgive is in the present moment. This is not the end of the journey; this is the beginning of a completely new way of life.

How will I experience my life in new ways?

You open the door to a new understanding of who you are as you discover your inner strength and your true self-love. From this place of emotional center, you begin to see your world with fresh eyes—eyes that do not judge yourself or others. Deep within, you understand that at this moment you are doing the best you can, yet so are all the other people in your life.

The present moment is where you are now, you are not in the past or in the distant future. It is here where you are the most aware and connected to the fullness of who you are. This is the place where your inner strength and self-love will be found. Your thoughts, words, and actions become a manifestation of your true self-love. To be in the present moment is to be connected with your true self and the love of all creation. Through this connection you begin to live in harmony, truth, and honesty with yourself and those in your life.

I can only live my truth in the present moment?

Think of the present moment as standing in front of an open door leading in to a room where everything is true and right for you. Here you will find all the loving guidance and wisdom you may ever need. You will also discover an endless flow of unconditional love. This is available to you as long as you remain centered, present, and true to yourself. In the here and now, you are connected with your authentic self—the truth of who you are. Through this connection, living and speaking your truth will bring more joy, love, and happiness in to your life. Living and speaking your truth is born from being completely honest with yourself about who you are, what you believe, and what you feel about the world around you.

Being in the present moment means you are not judging yourself for past mistakes or things that have not gone well in life. You are accepting yourself with love and compassion. While in the present moment you are saying to yourself, "Here I am right now, loving and accepting myself as I am."

What happens if I am focused and centered in the present moment, but the people around me are not?

Being in the present moment centers you emotionally. In this place of center, you are able to understand those around you better than if you were focused on the past or the future. Your continued focus on being in the here and now allows you to stay away from the negative conversations or comments of others. While staying centered, you naturally speak your truth with love and compassion. Knowing you are at your strongest in the present moment allows you to focus on how you are feeling. Then through this awareness you adjust your words and behavior to maintain your center. You find there is no need for you to become involved in any negative thoughts or words as you remain emotionally centered.

It's taking me some time to get a thorough understanding of the importance of being in the present moment.

There are times in your day when you are fully engaged in the here and now. Think for a moment when you are completely focused on the task at hand. Meditation is one place where your focus will be true and centered. If a person says they are in the "zone" and not to disturb them, they are focused on the present moment. When you understand you are at your strongest emotionally and true inner guidance flows to you unimpeded while in the present moment, it becomes easier to find your center. It is here you will connect with your inner peace.

In my busy day, what is the best strategy for staying in the present moment?

This is a question of focus. Ask yourself what are you focused on? What can you do to change your focus if it is not benefiting you? Can you make the changes allowing you to experience the wisdom and guidance found in the present moment? If things are not going well, you can shift your focus to something better, so you begin to experience your true self.

A simple way to change your focus could be to notice the beauty around you—maybe the clouds in the sky, or a flower you see as you go about your day. The idea is to change your focus away from past thoughts to something worth appreciating right now. Other examples might be watching the grace and beauty of a flock of birds, or thinking of a soothing piece of music, even the smell of an afternoon rain shower. Anything in your immediate experience that may help you find something to appreciate can place you in the present moment. If you learn to see the beauty around you, this will help you move in to a more centered awareness of the here and now.

When you accept that your inner self-love can be accessed in the present moment, it becomes your choice as to how you want to change your focus to experience this self-loving way of life. Your inner peace and wisdom come from within, yet they are at their most powerful while you are in the present moment.

THE MORE THINGS YOU FIND TO APPRECIATE, THE EASIER YOUR DAY WILL FLOW.

Appreciation

When you take an honest look at your life you may find many things to appreciate. Healthy food, good friends, warm shelter, to name just a few. These things bring a feeling of joy, happiness, and contentment in to your life. If you are not having a good day the act of appreciation can quickly improve your outlook.

For the people and things you enjoy in life, conveying appreciation is easy because it feels so good. Appreciation is a way of sharing love, kindness, and compassion. These positive emotions benefit anyone in need of an emotional boost. Who does not like an uplifting compliment, or a word of praise for a job well done?

What about you? When was the last time you expressed appreciation to yourself for a job well done or the way you handled a challenging situation? Is appreciating yourself difficult? Is it because you have been taught self-appreciation means placing yourself on the pedestal of believing you are better than others? What if self-appreciation was accepted as a powerful act of self-love? If you believe sharing kind words of appreciation will benefit others, then what about sharing these same kind and loving words with yourself?

Some aspects of your life are easy to appreciate while others are more challenging. Is it possible to appreciate the positive lessons found in negative experiences? Or can you appreciate the lessons taught to you by the people you find difficult to deal with? At times, appreciation can become a struggle when faced with certain challenges. Why should you appreciate those who have made your life difficult?

It may seem like an impossible challenge, to appreciate those who have caused hardship in your life. You may ask, "Why should I appreciate them? They hurt me!" A healthier life comes when you realize the people who caused your pain, have also created a desire within you for a better situation, whether it is for a specific outcome, or for a complete change of life. It is possible a life challenge could open new doors of opportunities previously unknown to you. Through your hardship you may have uncovered a hidden talent or a passion, possibly changing the direction of your life.

If you are courageous enough to find the positive lessons in any hardship you will grow stronger emotionally from the experience. You may have little control over the situation although you can learn to appreciate yourself by accepting you did or are doing your best. You can also release any negative self-judgement through the powerful act of self-forgiveness.

Appreciation helps you move closer to an awareness of your self-love and self-compassion. Through the act of appreciating your strength and courage while involved in challenging situations you can work your way to feeling better about yourself. As you recognize reasons to be appreciative you begin to experience more reasons to appreciate yourself and your life.

It's a challenge thinking about appreciating someone who has hurt me. How will appreciating them be beneficial?

Every person in your life is a teacher with important lessons for your emotional and spiritual growth. Even if they caused you pain, you have something positive to learn from them. If appreciating them is too difficult, then look within the experience to find the positive lesson and learn to appreciate the growth from the lesson.

One way to soften the pain is to appreciate yourself for doing the best you could during those uncomfortable times. Everyone is doing their best although it may not appear that way. There are reasons why people behave as they do, there may be hidden traumas in their life they have yet to heal within themselves.

When you were struggling with your painful situation, you were asking for a better experience. It is in this experience where appreciation can be advantageous to you, as well as finding the courage to forgive. The act of forgiveness may help you release any resentment or anger toward the other person. Once you have forgiven this person and moved on you may find appreciating the growth from the experience will benefit you throughout your life. You may never arrive at an emotional place to appreciate the person who hurt you, but it is the growth from the experience where you may find some level of appreciation.

If appreciating the person who hurt me is too painful, I should work to appreciate the learning and growth from the experience?

Appreciating someone who hurt you can be difficult. If you choose to forgive, you release them from your present consciousness. When you appreciate the positive growth from the experience, your focus shifts away from the negative situation, to one more positive and loving. The positive growth from a negative experience can be life changing. The point is to work toward focusing on and appreciating the positive aspects of the experience.

Finding the positive aspect of any situation will move you in a healthier direction emotionally. With this improved state of mind, you can quickly release the memory of the negative experience and begin to enjoy a better life.

What about severe pain and discomfort? In these situations, appreciation seems like a big challenge.

If you feel there is no need to search for the lessons from a painful experience, you may learn to forgive and move forward from there. Forgiveness is a powerful way to release you from dwelling on the past so you can refocus your attention on the present moment. This allows you to reach a healthier state emotionally. Through all you have experienced do not forget to appreciate yourself for the strength and courage it took to handle the emotional or physical pain you have lived through.

It is possible there could be a positive outcome from the situation that caused your discomfort. It may come in the form of an unseen opportunity benefiting you later in life. In the future, appreciating these hidden opportunities may help you overcome the discomfort you experienced.

If I get fired from my job, how can I see this as an opportunity I'll later appreciate?

Being fired from your job could be the push you need to start your own business, or a sign it is time to learn new skills, even move to a new location. When you discover the power of appreciation, you will see that everything that happens to you is a chance to improve your life. Appreciating these events as possible doorways in to a healthier life will change your focus to one more positive and loving.

I have to appreciate getting fired before I realize this could be a doorway toward a better opportunity?

It depends on how you react to your job termination. If you react with anger and frustration, you will find little in the way of opportunity and positive growth. On the other hand, if you react with a positive attitude and see this as an opening to a better future, you then recognize the value of the experience. This is where your learning and growth take place. Appreciation will carry you emotionally to a more self-loving and compassionate state of mind, thereby releasing your need for anger and frustration.

Imagine a positive opportunity as a gift someone left on your doorstep. You are unsure who sent it or why they sent it to you, yet you appreciate whoever they are. Opportunities are the same way. You appreciate the opportunity, even if you are unsure of the outcome. The opportunity will be a benefit if you view it from a positive perspective.

What if I am already in a good place emotionally, how does appreciation help me then?

If you are in a good place emotionally, expressing your appreciation can keep you in this good feeling place. No matter what is happening in the world around you, voicing your appreciation will elevate your state of mind. Speaking, thinking, or writing your appreciation is similar to speaking, thinking, and writing with love and compassion. As you begin to appreciate what you have in your life, you receive more wonderful experiences to appreciate. When you show your appreciation, you are taking the focus away from yourself, and turning this loving energy toward someone or something else. In doing so, you are radiating love and compassion out to the world.

Imagine appreciation as the energy you need to fuel your day. The more things you find to appreciate, the easier your day will flow, improving your attitude. You'll then discover even more to appreciate. Appreciation reveals to you more things to be thankful for. Through the act of appreciation you will find yourself in a happy, loving, and joyful state of being.

What if things aren't going well for me? Can I get to a healthier frame of mind through the act of appreciation?

Try to lift yourself to a better place emotionally by searching for things to appreciate. These may be small things at first, a flower along the sidewalk, a beautiful sunset, or something as simple as the food on your plate. Anything beneficial to your life experience can and should be appreciated at some point in your day.

What if all I have in the cabinet is peanut butter?

Then appreciate the peanut butter you have. If you only own a bicycle, then appreciate your bicycle. There are things in your life to appreciate once you see they have value to you. A flower along the sidewalk has value—it adds beauty to your day and the flower's strength is worth appreciating. When you appreciate what you do have, this places you in a positive position to see the value in what you have in your life. If you can appreciate the jar of peanut butter, you will surely appreciate the crackers on which to eat the peanut butter.

It seems when I appreciate what I have, I relax a bit and stop criticizing myself for what I don't have.

As you begin to appreciate what you have your focus shifts away from what you do not have. From this place of appreciation, there becomes no need to find fault with your life or yourself. You appreciate what you have, along with the life you are living. You no longer feel the need to criticize yourself for the lack you think is in your life. As you appreciate what you have, you're also telling yourself you approve of how you are handling the challenges in your life—you have begun to appreciate yourself with love and compassion.

Appreciating myself seems like an odd thing to do.

Appreciating yourself means accepting that you are always doing the best you can. There becomes no need to criticize yourself for the events in your day that may not have gone well. When you learn to appreciate yourself with self-love and self-kindness, you begin to recognize the truth of who you are. If appreciating yourself feels odd, it may be because you are denying yourself the inner love within you.

There is always a reason to appreciate yourself. The outcome of a better life can only be realized when you learn appreciation for yourself. This releases you from the harsh self-judgement that goes through your mind when things do not work out in your life. There can be no lasting life changes or accomplished desires if you do not appreciate yourself first.

Why will a desire not last or come to fruition, if I don't appreciate myself?

You are the center of all your dreams and true-life desires. Until you accept yourself with love and compassion you will continue to place the needs of others ahead of your own. In doing so, you are telling yourself you are not worthy of living a complete life. Appreciating who you are is acknowledging you have value to yourself. Your true desires have merit.

How does appreciating myself lead to valuing myself?

When you value something, a car, or a tool, you are more likely to maintain the item because you appreciate it. It is no different with yourself. When you appreciate your health you are more inclined to take better care of yourself. Through self-appreciation you begin to focus on what makes you emotionally and physically happy and healthy. If you are feeling rundown, or sick, it may come from a lack of self-appreciation. This is your way of telling yourself you are not worthy of experiencing your self-love and self-worth.

When I appreciate something, I value it?

When you are appreciating something or someone, you are adding value to them, you are recognizing their worth in your life. Have you experienced a situation where someone did not appreciate you? It is likely this awareness did not make you feel good or pleased with yourself. You may have felt many negative emotions from this experience. Conversely, by appreciating someone or something, you are showing your inner truth to those whom you are appreciating.

Is there a limit to the things I can appreciate in my life?

There are no limits to what is worth appreciating in life. As you acknowledge the aspects of your life worth appreciating, you discover more reasons to appreciate what you have and the people who are part of your life. Appreciation is limitless, yet it begins with an honest appreciation of yourself.

Do I have to appreciate everything about the people around me? I appreciate some aspects of them, but other aspects are challenging to appreciate.

All people have aspects worth appreciating. It is best to focus on what you do appreciate about them, rather than to focus on what makes them challenging. Think of the people in your life as teachers with important lessons for your emotional and spiritual growth. This will help you move to a state of mind that is more accepting and understanding. Through your appreciation of them, your interactions will go smoother, adding more positive energy to the relationship.

It may be a challenge to focus on what I appreciate about someone I don't agree with. How do I resolve this?

Would you rather focus on what makes you uncomfortable about them, possibly adding to your discomfort? Or would it be best to focus on what you can learn from them and begin to appreciate them for the positive lessons they are teaching? Challenging people are in your life for you to learn something. The lessons could be ones of tolerance, compassion, or appreciation. If there are people in your life you do not agree with, you could learn to observe the world through their point of view. This may give you more insight in to why you disagree.

Is it possible to appreciate what I do like about certain people and leave it at that?

If you do not learn the lessons you are meant to learn from these people these lessons will continue to reappear in your life. This means you will face other opportunities to learn these lessons in the future if you do not learn these lessons now. These people challenge you for a reason. When you find the reason, you will see the lessons clearly.

Can I appreciate someone I don't know?

Appreciating someone you do not know is easy. You may not have a preconceived idea of who you think they should be, so you may not have any judgement toward them. This allows you to appreciate what you may have in common rather than focus on your differences. You could appreciate how they are caring for their family or appreciate the skills they have. Appreciation is also an understanding that the other person, whether you know them or not, is doing their best. It makes no difference if they live on the next street, or halfway around the world. There is always something you can learn to appreciate about others.

What about people who want to hurt other people? What can I appreciate about them?

This can be a challenging situation. Appreciating someone who wishes to harm others is a person who is not connected to their true self-love or their inner voice. They may not be aware of the powerful guidance existing within them. In their place of tremendous discomfort, they are doing their best—even if it does not appear that way. They are struggling within themselves to find a better outcome, yet they are blind to the possibilities. They feel hurting other people is their only option to ease their inner struggle. Accept that all people are doing the best they can, even those who cause harm to others.

Learning to appreciate those who are different can pose some challenges.

You have more in common with the other people in the world than you may be willing to admit. Once you begin to accept this idea, learn to appreciate your commonalities, and leave your differences behind. If you find yourself judging them, you have turned your attention away from what you may have in common and are focusing on your differences.

If I learn to appreciate what I have in common with other people, will my relationships improve?

Seeing the commonalties you have with others clears the way for a better understanding of who they truly are, allowing your relationships to flow smoothly. When you focus on appreciation, you are radiating the energy of love and compassion the other person may feel. Through the positive mindset of appreciation, you may recognize the common ground you share with others, which could lead to healthier relationships.

All this because I am willing to find something to appreciate about myself and others?

True appreciation for those around you begins when you share your self-love without judgement, or expectations. You have found your inner happiness and joy because you are comfortable with who you are. This allows you to appreciate those who appear different from you but who may share commonalities with you. Through the act of appreciation, you lift the spirits of the people in your relationships, thereby improving the lives of everyone you come in contact with throughout your life.

Why does expressing my appreciation to someone feel uncomfortable?

In today's busy world appreciation is rarely expressed. Everyone is moving so quickly they feel there is little time for this courtesy. Also, the person who is your focus of attention may not be sure what to think of your appreciation. They may feel uncomfortable because they believe there could be an ulterior motive behind your act of kindness. This is because there is little spoken of the positive power of expressing your appreciation. Appreciation is a simple act of speaking your positive feelings toward another person. There should be no shyness or hesitation if your desire is to express your appreciation to others.

What do we do when people push our comment of appreciation aside, or use the comment to build their ego?

In either case there is a lack of self-love and self-worth. One person feels uncomfortable because they have not learned to accept a positive compliment. They may feel self-doubt or believe they are unworthy of your approval. A lack of self-love and feeling they do not deserve the appreciation could be the reason for their behavior.

The other person will gladly accept your appreciation, then use the comment to add to their higher sense of self-worth, thereby boosting their self-image. This is also showing a lack of self-love. They need the appreciation as a gauge to measure their self-worth. In both cases, there is a lack of self-love and little self-appreciation, though the reasons for their behavior are different.

If I turn down a compliment, I'm not experiencing my self-love?

In turning down a compliment, you are saying to yourself you are unworthy of accepting the appreciation being offered. Imagine a compliment of appreciation as a loving gift this person is giving you. When you turn down this gift, you are telling yourself you are not worthy of the love and compassion associated with the compliment. You put yourself down and deny yourself your true self-love when you refuse a comment of appreciation.

What happens when accepting a compliment of appreciation makes me feel powerful and proud?

If the appreciation boosts your self-esteem and self-worth, then this is also a case of experiencing a lack of self-love. Seeking the approval of other people for your self-worth will lead to an inner discomfort now and in the future. A compliment received this way can cause uncertainty in the person who has expressed the appreciation as well. In the future, they may stay silent, rather than cause discomfort within themselves, or the recipient of their appreciation.

What is the best way to show someone our appreciation?

The best way is to be true, sincere, and honest with your words. The positive energy from your intention will be felt by those you are appreciating. If they refuse your act of kindness it should not be your concern as to how they handle your appreciation. The best you can do is to speak words of love and compassion in your message of appreciation. How the recipient of your appreciation deals with the compliment is up to them. Whether they accept the appreciation or not, it is their choice.

I would like to return the conversation to self-appreciation. There are some aspects of myself I do appreciate, while other aspects not so much. How do I reconcile these differences?

When you focus on what you appreciate about yourself, you move to a more self-loving place. Also, the aspects of yourself you do not appreciate are a part of your being, these aspects make up who you are—positive or negative. Once you accept these less-than-ideal aspects of yourself, you can move to a more positive place emotionally, resulting in experiencing more self-love and self-worth.

Recognize that self-appreciation is an emotion that can, and will, build to become a powerful, positive emotion. Have the courage to examine what you do not appreciate about yourself. This helps you become more aware of why you behave as you do in certain situations. You may also learn this lack of self-appreciation is not based on your inner truth. These negative emotions are based on false beliefs along with the negative self-talk constantly repeated in your mind. False beliefs can create much discomfort within you as well. This discomfort is the difference between your truth and the false belief.

What is the difference between my inner truth and my false beliefs as they relate to self-appreciation?

Here is an example. You are having fun with friends you love. You are having a joyful, wonderful time, you feel this joy both physically and emotionally. There is no separation within you—this is experiencing your inner truth. However, if things are not going well, you will feel a level of discomfort. This discomfort is the separation or the difference, between your inner truth, and the false beliefs creating your experience.

When you say you have aspects of yourself you do not appreciate, it is because on these subjects, you have chosen to separate yourself from your inner truth and your self-love. In this case you may continue to believe something negative taught to you from a young age. Even the aspects of yourself you do not appreciate make up who you are. Learning to appreciate who you are, in all aspects of your life, is a selfish act of self-love. To experience your self-love, learn to appreciate yourself without guilt, shame, or judgement.

Why do the parts of myself I do not appreciate make me who I am?

The characteristics you choose not to appreciate affect your life and the people you encounter in your day. Through the reactions of others your world is shaped, whether they react positively or negatively toward you. What you do not appreciate about yourself causes a desire within you to improve these aspects of who you are.

The desire for a healthier life will cause emotional and spiritual growth within you, along with a better understanding of why you are unable to appreciate all aspects of your life.

What can I learn from the aspects of myself I don't appreciate?

If you have a desire for a healthier life and are willing to look at your life experiences with truth and honesty, you can begin to recognize the lessons these negative aspects hold. Once you learn the lessons, the aspects you do not appreciate will become part of your strengths.

There are more reasons to appreciate your life than you may think. All that is required is for you to trust in what you know to be honest and loving. As you learn to trust your inner voice and silence your negative self-talk, you will be able to release any false beliefs preventing you from appreciating who you are. This awareness will help you learn to appreciate a life filled with love and compassion.

ACCEPTING WHO YOU TRULY ARE IS THE ROAD TO INNER PEACE.

Acceptance

Is it possible to accept where you are in life, physically and emotionally? Do you accept the changes you see in the world, or do you struggle against them? Have you courageously accepted the people around you, even though they may not see the world as you do? Can you accept yourself for who you truly are?

Self-acceptance, as well as accepting those who are different than you—whatever their race, ethnic background, or religious beliefs, can be a challenge. Accepting an ever-changing world can also pose some uncertainty as well. If you have a difficult time accepting yourself, or the ever-changing world, where does this resistance originate? Could it be you judge yourself and those in your life as not doing enough or not being good enough?

Accepting who you truly are is the road to inner peace and an awareness of your self-love. Even though some people will point out your faults and shortcomings you can stay true to yourself through the love you found from self-acceptance. If you are subjected to a constant dialogue of the false beliefs of others you may begin to believe what they are saying, thereby accepting who they think you are, instead of recognizing your authentic self.

Learning to accept yourself takes a desire to understand what is true and right for you—learning your inner truth. Knowing this truth allows you to question your false beliefs and ignore the opinions of others regarding who they think you should be. You may begin to experience the person you are meant to be in this lifetime knowing this is your truth, by the love and compassion you feel each and every day. Now you may accept your authentic self while releasing from your consciousness the version of who you thought you were, the person who was constantly seeking the acceptance of others for your self-worth.

Self-acceptance is accepting yourself completely with love and compassion—without self-judgement or self-ridicule. This acceptance can be a new experience for people. Often there can be disappointment as you look in the mirror or see pictures of yourself. You may look at yourself with harsh judgement, thinking of all the physical and emotional traits you would like to change. Judgement will not lead to a self-loving acceptance. If you cannot accept yourself with love and compassion, then it will be impossible to accept other people as well. Accepting yourself is loving yourself enough to release your need to judge yourself and those in your life.

Every day you, and all people, are doing the best you can, accepting this powerful truth is the first step in recognizing the truth of who you are. This belief may be too simple or too challenging for some to accept. Yet, in an emotional place of self-doubt you will not find the clarity and focus needed to allow you to begin to enjoy the truth of who you are. Your doubt and judgement will limit your ability to be accepting of yourself and others.

Why don't I accept myself for who I am?

Do you measure yourself against the people around you or the unrealistic standards of society? If you judge yourself for not doing enough based on how others are living, you are not accepting that you are doing your best. This is the reason for any inner discomfort you may be experiencing. To accept yourself without negative self-judgement is to accept that at this moment, you are doing the best you can.

Accepting yourself is to acknowledge the eternal flow of love found within you. This love allows you to release any self-judgement you may have toward the choices you are making and the life you are living.

Isn't accepting myself just accepting I'm not good enough, then acknowledging I need to do better?

When you feel you are not good enough and believe you could be doing better, you are judging yourself harshly as you think these thoughts. It then becomes difficult to move forward to a place of comfort that will allow you to change your state of mind without self-judgement. You will never experience a complete life if you are judging yourself as being unworthy of the best life possible. It will be a struggle to accept yourself if you do not see yourself through the eyes of your own love and kindness.

What happens if I look in the mirror and see I need to get in better shape, or I'm upset with myself because I missed a promotion at work. Why is it so hard to accept myself with love and kindness?

A constant dialogue telling yourself you have fallen short on your appearance or a promotion at work will not lead to positive growth. There are only the negative feelings of not being good enough. First accept that you are doing your best. Then allow yourself to recognize and learn the beneficial lessons needed to move forward to a more positive self-image both physically and emotionally.

Here is a question for you. Have you ever tried to do your best work while someone is criticizing everything you are doing? It is not a comfortable experience. It is the same way if you constantly stay in the negative frame of mind and feed your negative self-talk with words of self-doubt and self-ridicule.

Accepting who I am now, may be different than how I was raised to see myself. Why the difference?

A person will often see themselves through the beliefs other people have taught them. You have learned who you may be is based on what other people think about you and not what you know to be true about yourself. Oftentimes, you accept their opinion of who they think you are, without question. Through this type of behavior, you begin to live a life based on what you think you should do, and who you think you could be, so you can maintain their view of who you are.

This could make my life uncomfortable, couldn't it?

The inner conflict between what is expected of you and the life you want to live can cause considerable emotional unrest within you. In this case accepting yourself can be difficult. Learn to focus on what makes you truly happy and what desires are right for you. Then work to discover the life path you know is true and right for you. Living life through the expectations of other people will be unsatisfying. This discomfort is telling you something in your life is amiss and changes need to be made for a healthier, more authentic life.

If I accept myself, yet still feel uncomfortable, what is this telling me?

This discomfort is telling you you're not following your true path. Accepting yourself is the way to an honest understanding of who you are. This truth will lead you to the complete life you are searching for. If you are living a life that is not your truth, not authentic, you will feel uncertain about the direction you are heading.

When you accept a life not in sync with who you are, or with who you are meant to be, you will feel some discomfort within you. This feeling is the separation between how you are living and the life you are meant to live.

There are times in your life when everything flows easily—your job, your relationships, and the choices you make. This is the union between your life and the life you are meant to live. You are in sync with who you are. When these experiences feel unsettling or dysfunctional, this is the separation between your inner truth and the life you are choosing to live. The discomfort is guidance saying you need to find your way to living your inner truth.

If I accept a life that isn't right for me, I'll know by how it feels?

If at first you accept a life that is not true and right for you, the discomfort will feel small, almost insignificant. As time goes on you feel more unsettled. For some reason you believe it may be too late to change course, so you accept this way of life. You may begin to think this is the way life is supposed to be, living with this constant uncertainty. The people around you are also living this way so there is no one you can talk with about your situation. You then accept this uncomfortable feeling as just the way life is. The uncomfortable feeling is telling you your current life situation is not right for you.

How will I know if I have made the right choices, or if I have accepted a life not in my best interest?

The way to know if your choices are right is to examine how you feel after the outcome of your decisions. Do you feel your choices were honest and true? Or have your choices made you uncomfortable? This is the most accurate way to tell if you have chosen the right course of action and have made the best choices leading to a complete life. Through this guidance you only accept what is right for you by paying attention to how it makes you feel.

Is there a connection between accepting what is right for me and accepting myself?

To accept yourself with complete honesty is to know what is always true and right for you and then to live by this new awareness. As you learn to trust your inner guidance in regard to how something makes you feel, you begin to accept your ability to trust what is true for you. You can then move in a positive direction by following this guidance and learning to accept who you truly are because of the love and compassion you now have for yourself.

If I trust my feelings and go in the direction that feels best, I'm accepting myself with love and compassion?

By trusting your feelings and the guidance you receive from your inner voice, you are accepting your choices as a priority in your life. This new way of living is accepting yourself without doubt or self-judgement. You have chosen to focus on what makes you truly happy thereby accepting that your desires have value to your happiness and well-being.

Does accepting other people in to my life fit in to this conversation?

Once you have accepted yourself with honesty and love, you are then able to accept other people in your life without condition or expectation. You also understand and accept that these people are doing the best they can with their life situations. Your love and compassion will take away any judgement that often exist in relationships.

Why is it a challenge to accept people who are different than we are?

You may be too intent on your differences rather than learning about what you have in common. Continued attention on your differences adds strength to the uncertainty and hesitation toward those who appear different than you. This negative energy prevents you from seeing your commonalities. Focusing on your differences will keep you from accepting them as you would like to be accepted by them.

How do we change this?

Stop focusing on your differences, then begin to recognize what you have in common. People have much more in common with those they disagree with than they are willing to accept. This is especially true when it comes to someone who is from a foreign country, speaks an unfamiliar language, or a person who appears to be less fortunate than you. Accepting a person for who they are is more loving and compassionate than not accepting them based on how they appear or the language they speak.

Why is it so difficult to accept people who are different than we are?

In a word, fear. You are afraid of them because they look different, eat different foods, and speak a language unknown to you. You cannot accept them because you know little about them and this makes you fearful. Thus, making it impossible for you to accept them as loving, caring, human beings.

A fear such as this can prevent us from accepting people just because they appear different than us?

This fear is unfounded and can be powerful in shaping the way you interact with those who are unlike you. Fear such as this is often taught from generation to generation throughout a family. In a short amount of time the initial reason for this fear and lack of acceptance has been forgotten or misunderstood, yet the fear is still taught to younger generations. There may be no truth in this fear, yet it is rarely questioned or challenged.

What is the best way to overcome this kind of fear, so we can move to a place of complete acceptance?

Fear is always accompanied with an inner feeling of discomfort. In this situation this powerful feeling shows you that you're not in sync with what you know to be true, right, and loving. Your authentic truth is one of love and compassion for all people, including yourself. This also includes people who look and speak differently than you. For a healthier understanding of what other people are going through focus on what you have in common. This can ease your fear and uncertainty.

All people want to be loved, have a dry shelter to protect them from the weather, healthy food to eat, and clean water to drink. These are basic needs, yet they are also something all people have as a common desire. Focusing on your commonalities, not your differences, will help you move past your fears in to a more loving, compassionate state of mind.

We may get to a place where we accept other people who are unlike us, but they may not accept us as easily. What can we do about this?

There is little you can do about what other people believe, or how they behave toward you. The best you can do is to speak your truth with honesty and integrity. This tells people who you are without compromising your true self. When you silence your truth with the intention of pleasing another person, there is no longer any lasting growth within the relationship. You have lowered yourself to a negative way of thinking and behaving. In doing so you have separated yourself from your authentic self.

Should I stay true to myself and not get involved in the negative thinking of other people?

There is no point in replacing your truth and your self-acceptance with the false beliefs of another person. This will cause an inner discomfort felt deep within you. Staying true to yourself is much more important than being accepted by someone else.

What if the issue with this other person is centered around my job?

Is your job worth substituting your inner truth with the false, negative beliefs of another person? If this is the case, you are sacrificing yourself—your inner truth—to please someone who does not accept you for who you are. Over time you may become bitter as a result of having made these changes to please this person. Accepting yourself means realizing the deep love you have for yourself, while remaining true to this love. No good comes from sacrificing your truth to please another person.

Our society has many inaccurate stereotypes that are not very accepting. How do we handle these issues if we are stereotyped by others?

Stereotypes are not a complete understanding of the people involved. Many times, stereotypes are based on a lack of true information. In dealing with this type of situation, it is best to remain your authentic self. If someone has placed you in a stereotype, it is not worth trying to conform to their expectations as a way to please them. Staying true to who you are and not giving them the power to stereotype you benefits you in these situations. You are at your strongest when you are courageous enough to accept yourself for who you truly are. While in this state of being you can stand strong if someone sees and treats you as a stereotype.

Are stereotypes a form of false beliefs and negative judgement?

Stereotyping people is a combination of judgement and false beliefs, not based on an honest understanding of the facts surrounding a certain person or a group of people. The person who is stereotyping is unwilling to accept you or this group of people for who they truly are. They are judging others from a place of false beliefs and limited knowledge. Much of the reason a person stereotypes another person is because they lack self-love.

Do I have to accept all the people who I encounter in my travels?

Which feels better, accepting them with love and compassion on your first meeting? Or judging them harshly based on what little you truly know about them and then attempting to form a relationship from this negative mindset? You may have felt this negative energy as you were being judged by someone on your first meeting. How did that make you feel? It is no different when you judge someone. They feel the negative energy of your judgement. They may recognize they are not being accepted by you, causing them to shut you out of their lives, emotionally and physically.

I'm beginning to understand that acceptance is an emotion which radiates energy other people can feel.

All beings are more aware of the energy people radiate than you may realize. It is because of this sensitivity you will know if you are being accepted by another person or not. This awareness was at one time a skill that could mean your survival.

Is it possible to accept myself with love and compassion yet stay in a life situation which is challenging and hard to accept?

If you know you are wanting a better life and you are moving in a positive direction—no matter how slowly it seems — you can accept yourself with love and compassion. But, if you are trying to accept yourself, while doing nothing to improve your life, this is not accepting who you are. You will not be able to love and accept yourself while staying in a negative situation that does not move you to a healthier, more loving place emotionally.

I can't love and accept myself if I choose to stay in a challenging situation?

Recognize the difference. In one situation, you are doing something to improve your life—this shows self-love and self-respect. In the other, you are doing nothing to improve where you are. The first example shows self-acceptance and a desire for self-improvement. The other shows an absence of both. To truly accept yourself is to give yourself every opportunity to succeed in all aspects of your life.

In one case, you are doing something to change your life. This is an easy thing to accept with self-love. In the other, you are not following your inner guidance which will lead you to living a complete life. Instead, you are choosing to stay in an undesirable situation. You have a role to play in finding happiness and joy in your life.

Accepting yourself begins with taking on this responsibility. From there, it becomes your mission to believe in yourself with truth and honesty. You choose to do something to improve your life, and then accept responsibility for the outcome of your decisions—whatever the results. In this mindset, it becomes easy to accept who you are because your life is yours to live as you desire. Accepting responsibility for your life is accepting yourself with love and compassion.

Why is accepting responsibility for myself accepting myself with love and compassion?

It is through self-love and compassion where you recognize your responsibility for maintaining your happiness and your self-worth.

You cannot leave this responsibility to others. When you accept that your life has significance, your true needs and desires become a priority to your happiness.

I have injured myself recently. Why do I keep reliving the situation and the emotional pain from this experience?

There is much second-guessing along with self-doubt surrounding a situation such as this. These negative emotions keep you in the moment of injury and prevent you from being in the present moment. As a result, you are not accepting the fact that you were doing the best you could at the time. By refusing to accept your situation you are limiting your ability to heal. Even if your injury heals, your constant focus on the moment of injury keeps you emotionally in the painful past. Your healing begins when you focus your energy on healing instead of the moment you injured yourself.

I have been second-guessing myself, is it because I am unable to accept where I am as a result of the injury?

Being unable to accept where you are emotionally keeps you in a negative frame of mind. Consequently, there is little room to move forward as you continue to relive the painful experience. Releasing these negative thoughts and emotions through self-forgiveness allows you to begin to accept your new reality as a result of your injury.

As we age our body changes. Will accepting these changes make aging easier for us?

Comparing the physical body you have today with the body you had in the past, limits the possibilities available to you now. Each stage of a person's life will have physical and emotional changes. You could look at these changes as a positive or negative experience—the choice is yours. If you accept the body you have and release your thoughts of the body you once had, you will experience your present moment with more joy and self-love. Where you are now, physically and emotionally, is where you have the most strength and stamina to handle what life has to offer. If your focus is on what you had in the past, you may miss an opportunity in your present experience.

Do I have to accept my knees hurt and my back is not as strong as it once was?

If this is the choice you choose to make, then this is what you can expect from your life in the future. Yet, if you accept the health you have and are appreciative of your present moment, you will arrive at a mindset of self-acceptance. This mindset will not allow your back or knees to define who you are.

People resist the changes that occur throughout their lives, whether they are physical or emotional. This resistance is based on what they have experienced throughout their past, not on what they are appreciating and accepting about themselves now. Often people are too focused on their past health to be appreciative of the health they are experiencing today.

Accepting myself in a quickly changing world can be unsettling.

Imagine self-acceptance as a solid foundation built on self-love. No matter what is happening in the world around you, you have a solid foundation of unshakable self-love supporting you. The world may be changing, but you are steadfast in your self-acceptance. The ever-changing world does not have the strength to challenge the truth of who you are.

There is little you can do to stop the world from changing. Yet you can learn to accept that you and everyone else are doing their best, given what you know right now. Accepting others and the world around you begins with accepting the truth of who you are and then living this truth with honesty, integrity, and love.

THIS IS THE TRUTH OF WHO YOU ARE.

Your Authentic Truth

What does it mean to experience your authentic truth? Is being an authentic person necessary for living a complete life? Can you maintain your authentic self while you change and grow emotionally from the challenges you have faced? Is it possible to look within yourself to find the answers to these questions to help you discover your authentic truth?

During the course of your life, you have been asked to be a different person for different people: brother, sister, lover, teacher, mother, friend. The question is, "Who are you, to you?" Would you consider yourself your own best friend—your own confidant? Are you comfortable being by yourself, or do you need a crowd of people to support you? Do you see yourself as being authentic?

What does being authentic even mean? In short, being your authentic self means discovering your truth, then living by this truth. From this powerful awareness, you can express your truth to the people you encounter in your life. Living a complete life is living by your authentic truth—the truth that only you know is right for you.

If you are focused on pleasing those around you to boost your self-worth or you are bitter because you have sacrificed your dreams for the needs of others you may not be living an authentic life. Placing the needs of other people ahead of your own needs may have caused you to give up much of your authentic truth. Other factors keeping you from living an authentic life would be believing the false beliefs you have learned throughout your life, as well as accepting the negative self-talk you hear in your head as the truth.

An authentic life begins when you connect with the constant stream of loving guidance flowing within you, leading you to your true self-love. There becomes no need to seek the approval of those around you to boost your self-worth, because you now feel the depth of this inner love. This love is authentic, it is purely you. It has always been within you, only now you are allowing yourself to feel and experience this love. This love is real, this love is true.

Once you recognize this love, your inner trust will strengthen, and because of this, you will have the courage to live an authentic life, a life knowing your inner self-love, and then choosing to live by this love. This will weaken your self-doubt and begin to silence the negative self-talk often repeated in your daily experience, thereby allowing you to enjoy the best life has to offer. If for some reason events do not work out the way you had planned, stay centered within your inner love and remain true to your authentic self. There becomes no need for self-judgement—or the judgement of other people for that matter—knowing your authentic self speaks and lives focused on the tremendous love found within.

Why is living an authentic life important?

Living an authentic life is important because this is the truth of who you are. You recognize you are not the false beliefs you have accumulated over time. In the act of living an authentic life, you begin living your inner truth without doubt or hesitation. It is important, because by living your authentic life you will experience the world as you may never have experienced it before. Your true self-love radiates out to those around you. From your awareness of this love, you will feel love and compassion returned to you, from those you meet in your day. Life will change because you are now speaking with honesty and truth, living your life based on this authenticity.

It seems I'm living a fine life without all the effort of finding my authentic self.

This false belief is based on a limited view of what your life could be like. The life you are experiencing now is unlike the unlimited life you could be living if you began to accept the truth of who you are and the inner growth that comes from knowing this truth. There may be some effort to sift through your false beliefs and discard those that do not align with your authentic self. This helps you begin to accept who you are meant to be. Yet this effort has more benefits than staying where you are in the unfulfilling place of a fine life.

If I release my false beliefs, then begin to accept who I am with love and compassion, will I begin to live an authentic life?

An authentic life is founded on speaking and living your truth in all aspects of your life. You cannot live an authentic life while you continue to judge yourself or criticize others. The contradiction of being in a negative place emotionally while assuming you are living an authentic life will cause you too much inner discomfort. To live an authentic life you must be living your true beliefs with love, compassion, and kindness. You must also accept that everyone is doing their best and you have no need to judge them. There should be no separation between your loving inner truth and the life you are living.

Is living an authentic life, all or nothing?

To live an authentic life is to accept all aspects of who you are with love and compassion. You can release the false beliefs that do not serve you any longer, then put an end to the negative self-talk preventing you from living a complete life. It is your choice whether to accept your complete self with love or not. In your desire for a better life you begin to move past the falsehoods you once believed were your truths to a more self-loving place within yourself.

How does working to live a more authentic life benefit me?

The desire to live an authentic life allows you to experience a part of yourself that may have been unknown to you in the past. You may begin to recognize the truth of who you are for the first time.

Through this new knowing you feel what makes you truly happy, you will no longer place this responsibility on someone else. Also, you begin to experience your true self-love. This is the love of your inner voice, guiding you to the best life possible, thereby allowing you to live a life you once thought was out of reach.

What if living an authentic life changes the way I have been living?

If the changes are slight, you have been living close to your authentic truth. If the changes are radical, then this shows you that you have been disconnected from your inner guidance, the truth this guidance speaks, and the life that will bring you lasting happiness. To work toward living an authentic life, is the work of living to the fullness of who you are. You and everyone in your life benefits from your commitment to this inner work.

Will living an authentic life make me happy?

In this new awareness you discover that the love you have been seeking from other people has always been within you. You can now release the false beliefs that have kept you from living an authentic life. As you let go of these false beliefs and your need for the approval of others you begin to feel what is true and right for you. You will also begin to experience your own inner truth that this is who you are and who you are meant to be in this lifetime. There is no need to sacrifice your desires or to place the needs of other people ahead of your own needs. Because of your new awareness you will begin to live your life based on love and compassion. Your happiness now originates from this place of love and truth.

Is it possible to live an authentic life if I place the needs of those around me second to my own needs?

To place your needs first means your health and well-being have become the main focus of your life. Conversely, if you place your health and your well-being second to those around you, you're implying you are not worthy enough to give yourself your full attention. With this behavior, you may not be taking care of yourself as you should.

Prioritizing yourself does not mean you leave the people around you without care or consideration. When you place your needs as an important priority, you will not feel any resentment when you help those around you. If you take care of yourself first, you will have the positive energy of your self-love to take care of those in your life without resentment or bitterness. Living an authentic life means being honest, kind, and compassionate with yourself and others.

Trying to figure out what is best for me in a complicated world is challenging. How will I know if it is right for me?

You will know if it is right by how the thought of it makes you feel. Does the idea bring you joy, happiness, and a feeling of excitement? Or does the idea make you feel uncomfortable, unable to move forward because you feel as if your feet are stuck in the mud?

You know an idea may bring temporary happiness, yet will this idea bring you true, lasting happiness? The true happiness that is more powerful—felt deeper within you—than the superficial happiness commonly experienced in a challenging world.

Do you sense a connection within yourself that makes you feel tremendous joy and unlimited love? This is the feeling you are seeking in the physical world, so you can live an authentic life.

How does this feeling in the physical world make me happy within myself?

Through the awareness of what makes you happy in the physical world, you begin to learn how genuine happiness feels. Then you can examine your life to see what brings you this feeling of deep joy and happiness and what does not. From there, look at your life to see what you would like to change for a more self-loving and compassionate experience.

There are things in my past that have prevented me from experiencing happiness. How do I handle these issues?

A constant focus on your past prevents you from experiencing happiness in the present moment. Your past has created who you are today, yet you do not have to let your past define who you are any longer. No matter what your history, it has not changed your authentic self. This authenticity is rooted deep within you and is not affected by your physical past. You can forgive yourself for the way you behaved in your past, this allows you to move forward toward an authentic life experience.

How does my past not affect my authentic self?

The past is a series of events in the physical world that often impact the way you experience the present moment. Your authentic self is an inner truth deeply rooted in love, kindness, and compassion; it is not affected by events in the physical world. This is who you are meant to be. As people focus on their past, they allow these events to alter the course of their lives. In doing so they separate themselves from their true desires, ambitions, and authenticity.

Even though my life has changed through a powerful negative event, it doesn't change my authentic self?

Negative events happen in the physical world. Your authentic self is found in the inner world of your true self. This inner world is filled with self-love and self-compassion. Knowing your authentic self is always within you allows you to move away from the negative experiences to a place of comfort, a comfort supported by self-love which begins with self-forgiveness.

A negative event can have such strength it may change the course of your life if you allow it to do so. However, you can regain your self-worth and the courage to move forward, through the act of forgiveness, and then focusing on finding your inner happiness. You will know what is right for you by whether it makes you feel love and joy, or sadness and frustration. These feelings of love and joy are found within the authenticity of who you are—not in negative experiences.

How does self-forgiveness help me experience my authentic self?

You cannot control many of the negative experiences happening in your life. What you can control is how you integrate the lessons from these events in to your present moment. Self-forgiveness allows you to release the pain of these events from your consciousness. From there, you begin to accept the love you have for yourself, moving you closer to experiencing your authentic self.

Why do the negative events in my life keep me from experiencing my authentic self?

Once a negative event happens you may blame yourself for not speaking up or not asking for help from those around you. As time goes on, self-blame builds in strength, thus increasing the distance between who you are in the physical world and your authentic self. Releasing these negative events through forgiveness is a compassionate act of self-love; one that gives you the strength and courage to accept your authentic self.

This acceptance allows you to live the life you are meant to live. Accepting yourself begins with releasing the false beliefs you have allowed to form your life and then silencing the negative self-talk keeping you from moving forward toward your true desires. It may be uncomfortable to consider that accepting who you are may change your life yet understand this change will be for your benefit—increasing your inner happiness, as well as your love for yourself.

I'm concerned that by accepting my authentic self, my life may change. How do I handle these changes?

The changes may not be as dramatic as you think. When you learn to accept your authentic self, you begin to feel more comfortable with who you are. There is no need to create a persona with the intention of pleasing others. These changes will feel right, as if you have known what you wanted your entire life, but only now are allowing yourself to fulfill these dreams.

These changes could be as simple as finding a job more in line with what makes you happy on a deeper level. Or as radical as moving to the country to raise livestock, living on a farm, or going to college at any age to earn a degree. The changes that occur in accepting your authentic self are changes that would not need to happen if you had been living and accepting your authentic self from a young age. If there is any change in your life it would be because you have been denying your authentic self to guide you through life, thereby living a life you were not meant to live.

Accepting a life I was not meant to live is a powerful statement.

People accept an idea of themselves taught to them from a young age. The idea of who they thought they were, was based on the opinions and false beliefs of other people. This then becomes the version of who they think they are even though it is not based on what they may feel is right for them. The strength and impact of these false beliefs have the capability to last an entire lifetime.

There needs to be a desire in a person's life to question their own beliefs before any changes can be made. An evaluation of these beliefs will reveal if they have been living a life not in alignment with the truth of who they are. A continued search within for their inner truth will lead them to their authentic self. Their lives will change for the better as they accept themselves for who they now know themselves to be. This new self-awareness will be based on the realization of their inner truth and their self-love. Their self-worth is now founded on the acceptance of their authentic self.

It may be difficult to question the beliefs we have held throughout our lives.

The intention of a journey of self-discovery is to connect with the truth of who you are and the self-love that is the foundation of your authentic self. Once this journey is begun, there becomes a willingness to ask yourself questions about your beliefs and then listen for the answers that free you from the limitations the false beliefs place on you. Through these answers, you begin to learn who you truly are. Now you can set out to live life in a deeply meaningful, authentic way.

How will a person differentiate the right answers from their negative self-talk?

They will know by the way the answers make them feel. The right answers have a foundation rooted in true love, kindness, and compassion. Negative self-talk is just, negative. If the questions are answered honestly, a person will feel the truth and love in the answer. If, for some reason, a person then denies the answer, they will feel a level of inner discomfort within themselves. They will be denying themselves the guidance to live their best life possible and their authentic self as well.

Why has the word "true" been used so often in this conversation?

Many people believe their negative self-talk and false beliefs are true because they have no other point of reference, and they have not taken the time to question these thoughts. They fail to realize a true belief is one founded in love and honesty. Any other thought or belief is not true and should be questioned and then discarded from one's consciousness.

There are false beliefs in a person's life that have tremendous strength. Questioning these beliefs may threaten the foundation of their life. It may be easier to agree with the false belief because the idea of change causes too much fear and uncertainty within this person.

You will know what is true for you because of an inner knowing that cannot be distorted by fear or uncertainty. As you begin to experience an authentic life, you will sense what is true for you and discover there is no other way to live. There will be an honesty within you that you learn to feel and trust.

This would mean learning that I could be a completely different person than I thought I was.

There could be a shift in your consciousness as you begin to experience the truth of who you are now, as you move away from who you thought you were. Once you begin to discover who you truly are, you will feel more self-love and self-worth than you have been experiencing in the past. Imagine the process of relearning who you are as a puzzle. When you begin to experience your authentic truth the pieces of your life begin to fit together easily, without question or hesitation.

There have been times in my life when everything seemed to flow smoothly—my job, relationships, you name it, it all flowed easily. Then there are other times nothing fits, and life is a struggle. Why are the differences so dramatic?

When your life flows smoothly, this is a sign you are on the correct path, living your authentic life. If nothing is working out for you, this is telling you changes must be made to get back on track to live a more truthful, authentic experience. When you examine the way your life is progressing you will know if you are on the path to discovering your authentic self. Struggle and hardship are important teachers, communicating lessons you need to learn to live a true and authentic life.

Whether life is flowing smoothly, or a struggle, there will always be learning that is beneficial to our growth?

Either way there will be learning. These experiences will be very powerful if you recognize them as lessons. People are unaware of the importance of discomfort within their lives. Discomfort, joy, happiness, and sorrow are all emotions revealing something about your present situation. The feeling of uncertainty is a message saying you may need to reevaluate the decisions you have been making.

Discomfort from within tells you that you have separated yourself from your inner truth and your inner guidance, which are always directing you to what is true and right. It is important to learn what messages your emotions are sending, because they are significant as you seek your authentic truth.

I may disappoint other people as I become more aware of my authentic self. How do I handle this?

The path to your authentic self is a path of finding the truth of who you are, then living by this authentic truth. The goal in accepting your authentic self is to experience a life filled with inner self-love and honesty. Your main focus should be to find your inner truth; this will move you closer to experiencing your authentic self.

The concerns of those around you may have caused much confusion throughout your life as you worked to conform to who they think you should be. By discovering your authentic self, you do not need to change who you are to please others. You love yourself enough to remain true to who you are. This may seem selfish, yet it is a selfishness based on finding what is right for you through experiencing your inner truth.

It sounds as if I shouldn't care what those around me think as I search for my authentic self?

At some point you must accept that your life and fulfilling your true desires are more important than what other people think. You do not want to hurt them or cause any disappointment. Yet as you begin to experience your authentic self, you then radiate the tremendous love you have discovered within yourself. The joy and happiness you experience from realizing your authentic self will ease any discomfort those around you may have had toward your life changes.

The people around me will feel the love I have for myself if I am living an authentic life?

When you begin to discover your authentic self, you experience an inner self-love you may never have experienced before. From this self-loving place those around you will feel that you love yourself, have self-worth, and self-compassion. Being with the people you love is radiating love to those around you. This is the power of discovering your authentic self, when you love yourself and others, without condition, or expectation. You love for the joy of being loving.

What if I have a passion that makes me feel wonderful every time I engage in the activity, yet the rest of my life is not as wonderful. Is my passion part of my authentic life?

Your passion is the starting point of an understanding of what an authentic life feels like. In your connection to your passion you are receiving guidance from your inner voice without doubt or hesitation. The guidance you receive while engaged in your passion is based on the complete love and trust you have for yourself. The wonderful feeling you experience while involved in your passion is your closest connection to your authentic self. If you are not feeling the same way in other aspects of your life, this is telling you that you may need to adjust those parts to regain this wonderful feeling.

People do not believe they have the ability to live an authentic life because their job or passion takes up too much of their focus. Your passion will flow easier as you learn to focus on living a completely authentic life. There is a false belief that a person who has a passion must live a life filled with struggle and hardship, to fan the flames of creativity. Many successful, passionate people live this way, so it is easily accepted. A complete and authentic life is one that experiences the wonderful feeling of love throughout the entire day, not only while engaged in a passion.

The feeling I experience while engaged in my passion is the feeling I should try to maintain throughout my life?

This feeling is based on trusting your inner honesty. While you are focused on your passion, the pathways to your authentic self are free from obstruction. You know what is right by how it makes you feel. You then move in that "good feeling" direction, without doubt or hesitation. When you begin to experience this feeling while in your everyday life, you are on the path to an authentic life.

What is the connection between my passion and an authentic life?

While engaged in your passion, you are allowing the loving guidance of your inner voice to be heard and you have learned to trust this voice. The intention is to allow this voice to guide you through all aspects of your life. Your passion is uniquely you, and so is the guidance spoken through your inner voice. This is the voice of your authentic self. As with your authentic self, no other person can experience your complete life as you do. This is the power and joy you will experience as you open yourself to living your authentic life.

What if I don't have a passion to experience this inner connection? How will I know if I am living an authentic life?

To know if you are living an authentic life—whether by intention or not—is to recognize that all aspects of your life are flowing smoothly from one to the next. There will be more joy and happiness in your life than sadness and frustration. The world will open up to you as you allow yourself to speak and live your truth. You now feel an inner connection with your true self and this connection radiates love out to the world around you.

Through the joy and love you now feel, you will know what is right for you at all times. Because of this awareness, you will know without a doubt if the life you are living is the life you were always meant to live. As you begin to live an authentic life, you will know what makes you happy and the responsibility for your happiness is yours and yours alone. Living an authentic life is the greatest gift you can ever give yourself because living an authentic life is the gift of pure self-love.

LIVING A TRUTHFUL, HONEST LIFE.

A Complete Life

Throughout this book topics have been presented for you to contemplate long after you have finished reading. With this final chapter, the intention is to discover how your life can improve emotionally, physically, and spiritually as you strive to live a complete life.

What does living a complete life mean and why is it important? A complete life is knowing the truth of who you are and then living the life you were always meant to live - one filled with love, joy, and happiness. No person is meant to live a life as anything other than their true authentic self.

There are people who do not live honest or complete lives. When this occurs, there is a separation between the life a person is experiencing and the life they have always wanted to live. This disconnect originates from not being aware of their inner guidance and their true self-love. The life they are experiencing may appear to be fine yet living a complete life will exceed any expectation of how fulfilling life could be. A complete life is just that, a life complete in all aspects: relationships, spiritual, emotional, physical, professional, and most importantly, your true self.

Living a complete life is accepting full responsibility for your own inner happiness and the outcome of your actions. You also accept responsibility for the decisions you make in your everyday activities. Decisions ranging from your health to your friendships to the love and compassion you are willing to share with those around you. No aspect of your life should be left unattended if the desire is to live a complete life.

While living a complete life, you learn to accept that your happiness is your main priority. You choose to accept this responsibility, and do not leave it up to other people to maintain your happiness. As you begin to enjoy your inner happiness, you have the courage to accept the truth of who you are and then allow others to be who they are, without criticism or judgement. You become aware of the choices you make between compassion and condemnation. One is based in love and respect, while the other is based on fear or judgement.

As you begin to live a complete life, you recognize there is no need to think negative thoughts or express hurtful words. You know this behavior is a disservice to you and those around you. When you become comfortable with your authentic self you will learn to trust your loving inner voice and now choose to speak and act with love and kindness. This is who you are meant to be. You can share your inner love without fear, hesitation, or judgement with everyone you encounter, even those who challenge you emotionally.

Living a complete life teaches you to trust your inner guidance, allowing you to say the true and loving words those around you are meant to hear. You begin to trust yourself while making the correct, loving decisions needed to live a complete life. There becomes no need for emotional reactions based on anger or skepticism. Instead of overreacting, you trust your true self-love, as it guides you to say and do the right thing.

The emotional needs you once asked others to satisfy will be found within you while living a complete life. From this loving awareness, you now move through the day radiating an inner confidence. Living a complete life means you do not need the constant emotional support of others to maintain your self-worth. You ask only their friendship as you choose to share your love with them without condition or expectation.

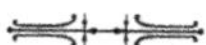

My life seems acceptable. Why is it important to live a complete life?

Living a complete life is important because in doing so you begin to experience the fullness of your authentic self. This allows you to live without the opinions of other people influencing your judgement, affecting your self-love, or challenging your self-worth. Love, joy, and kindness are now the foundation of all your interactions with others.

A complete life is living a truthful, honest one in every aspect of your daily experience. Your true self will be discovered without self-doubt or self-judgement. Most importantly, you will be living a life trusting the guidance of your inner voice knowing and experiencing your true self-love.

People may see themselves through the opinions of those around them, yet this is not an honest representation of who they are. Their self-image is based on what other people think not on what they know to be true and right for them. However, in their desire to live a complete life, they will begin to recognize their true selves. They can now leave the opinions of other people behind as they begin to live by their inner truth.

I'm fine where I am. Why go through all the work of trying to live a complete life?

If you enjoy your "fine" life and don't mind staying where you are emotionally, then you have a choice. You may choose to do the inner work so you can live a life that exceeds your expectations, or you can stay where you are emotionally. You must have a desire for an improved life before you begin to experience the benefits of living a complete life. If there is no desire for improvement, then your life may fall short of what a complete life has to offer.

How is living a complete life going to affect my relationships with my friends and family?

The more important question is, how will living a complete life change your relationship with yourself? Living a complete life gives you the courage to speak and live your truth. You no longer need to change who you are to please those around you. Nor will you be asking others to change who they are to please you. You now move past the need for the approval of others to boost your self-esteem, because you are living a self-loving life. When you begin to honestly speak your truth, without the fear of judgement or ridicule, your relationships are going to change to ones more loving, kind, and understanding.

It sounds as if I won't need anyone else in my life if I am living a complete life. Is this the case?

Living a complete life means you are not asking those around you to prove your self-worth or to justify your value to them. You no longer need to seek their love as a measure of your happiness. Living a complete life causes you to accept that your life is your responsibility to live with love and compassion. The people around you are now a loving part of your life not the foundation of your identity for which you have been asking them to provide in the past.

I'll be able to maintain my relationships with my friends, yet I will not need their approval to boost my ego, self-esteem, or self-worth?

Your need to live life supported by your ego will fade, as your true, loving, compassionate self becomes who you share with the world each day. Your self-worth is now bolstered by the love in your heart, not by your need for validation from your friends.

Is it possible living a complete life could change my relationships?

Your relationships could change for the better. By living a complete life, you are no longer asking those around you to be who they are not. In living this way, you accept others for who they truly are, without asking them to behave in a way that constantly pleases you.

If your relationships do change in a drastic way, then these relationships may not have been established on trust, love, and honesty. There was little room for growth or personal expansion within these relationships. If for some reason living a complete life ends a relationship know that healthier, more supportive relationships will come in to your life.

Wanting to live a complete life seems selfish, is this correct?

The answer to this question may challenge your definition of selfishness. Living a complete life is a selfish act of self-love. The reason for this is because you selfishly want to connect with your inner truth, and then speak and live by this truth. Living a complete life is about your desire to know your true self and then expressing this truth to the world.

To discover your inner love, strength, and courage is to live a complete life. This will be how you share your authentic self with all those around you, without condition or expectation. Is it selfish to want the best life possible?

I'm thinking about living a complete life, then sharing my life with those I encounter in my day.

As you begin to experience your self-love, you soon discover this love is the pathway to living a complete life. There is no need to ask other people to be responsible for your happiness because you have learned that your true happiness comes from within you.

The negative attitudes of others will no longer affect you as they may have in the past. You begin to recognize that people are responsible for their own happiness and you do not have to become involved in their discomfort as a way to make them feel better. When you speak with love and compassion you are helping others by being your authentic self, while staying positive without becoming involved in their negativity.

Is it best to stay in a positive frame of mind when I'm trying to help others with their situation?

Staying positive is the healthiest thing you can do for yourself as well as those who are experiencing any emotional or physical discomfort. When you are true to yourself and in a positive frame of mind, you have unlimited access to your inner strength, compassion, and wisdom. Through living a complete life you choose to stay positive by thinking and speaking your inner truth of love and kindness.

Can we live a complete life, while living through a negative experience?

To live a complete life is to become aware of your emotions as guidance. This guidance gives you the inner strength to minimize the impact negative circumstances have on your well-being. The situation may be negative, yet your attitude toward the circumstances will stay positive thereby giving you the best opportunity to resolve the situation quickly.

Is it possible to stay away from negative situations?

It would be impossible for people to stay away from negative situations. These experiences are opportunities for emotional growth and conscious expansion. It is best for you to stay in the powerful place of thinking and speaking with love and compassion. That way, negative experiences cannot control you emotionally as they may have in the past.

When I begin to live a complete life, negative experiences will no longer move me off my emotional center to an uncomfortable place?

When you begin to live a complete life, you will have the inner wisdom to recognize negative situations as learning experiences. This takes the negative energy away from the experience and keeps you focused on a positive frame of mind. Remaining centered in negative situations allows you to understand your strengths and identify what you would call your "weaknesses."

Aren't our "weaknesses" just issues we need to overcome in our lives?

Most people are taught that they have strengths and weaknesses. They choose to focus on their strengths and then work to improve their weaknesses -- although your strengths and weaknesses are what make you unique in the world. Your weaknesses are also a part of your strengths. If you believe them to be a weakness or a personal failing, then they have the ability to hinder your emotional growth.

If you accept your weaknesses as part of who you are, they then become a part of your strengths. The reason for this is because you now see them clearly without the need for self-judgement. Honestly accepting something about yourself you once thought was a weakness is creating a positive awareness that at one time may have been unknown to you. Focusing on the positive aspects of your "weaknesses" may cause tremendous growth within you.

If I change the negative view I have of my weaknesses to one more positive, my weaknesses then become part of my strengths?

Your "weaknesses" help create the entirety of who you are. They may be aspects you would like to improve or release from your consciousness. Once you recognize your weaknesses, they have less control over your life. They are now seen as opportunities for tremendous emotional growth. In doing so you become focused on your experiences—good or bad—in a positive manner. You no longer have the need to judge parts of yourself as negative or positive. This acceptance comes from a place of self-love, and your desire to live a complete life.

To live a complete life, I have to accept all aspects of who I am?

You can now accept yourself with love. There will be no need for harsh self-judgement because you have come to accept the fullness of who you are. When you reach this level of acceptance, you have the strength to ignore any self-doubt, or release your false beliefs, and silence your negative self-talk. Then you will begin to live in a way where you accept yourself as a whole person emotionally, physically, and spiritually.

In our society it's easy to find someone who will tell you what is wrong with your life and then recommend ways on how you should improve it. Why have I yet to hear anyone speaking of living a complete life?

Few people speak of living a complete life because few people understand the journey to living a complete life. Living a complete life is about accepting who you are without judgement or prejudice. In this awareness, you no longer need the opinions of other people to bolster your self-esteem or self-worth. This powerful experience is rarely spoken of because few people ask themselves who they truly are or if they are living the life they have always wanted to live.

You may have a negative reaction if someone tells you how you should change your life. If this advice continues, the negativity may cause you to doubt yourself or question the direction of your life. You may be living your life as a result of how you reacted to what others have said to you. In this case, you are not in control of your life, your life is controlling you. However, by living a complete life, you begin to take control of your life by accepting your responsibility for your choices. Thereby living life through your true desires and the honest decisions you make for your own well-being.

Why does "take control of your life," sound like an ego-driven statement?

Taking control of your life is as simple as changing what you want for lunch to something healthier or as challenging as moving to another location with the intention of finding a better career. When you take control of your life, you no longer allow your ego to control your destiny. You will be making loving choices based on what feels true and right for you.

The intention is to replace your negative self-talk with kind, loving, and encouraging words. It is also discovering what makes you happy on a deep inner level. Then moving in that direction, trusting yourself no matter what other people say about the life changes you are experiencing. These changes may be simple or they may be radical. It all depends on how much distance there has been between the life you are living and the life you are meant to live. Taking control of your life means ignoring people who tell you how you should live. By taking control of your life, you start to learn what is authentic for you.

If I take control of my life, I'll have to trust myself with every choice I make.

This is true. You will learn to trust what is true and right for you, emotionally as well as physically, as you never have in your past. Every aspect of your life becomes your responsibility. When you accept responsibility for living a complete life, you experience your inner self-love, and the truth of who you are.

I know people who are afraid of taking control, or responsibility for their lives. What advice is offered to them?

The best advice is, try to accomplish small, positive shifts first. This builds self-confidence and trust in how to make healthier, self-loving decisions. As they move forward accomplishing larger tasks their courage and self-esteem will build. In time they may not have to put much thought in to accomplishing a task, they may notice they completed it without much hesitation. People learn to trust themselves, as they grow emotionally stronger throughout this process.

How does this fit together with living a complete life?

Few people know their true desires. They may try new foods, different careers, even searching for the right life partner; it may take a few tries. It is the same way with living a complete life. There is going to be trial and error, or better said, trial and learning. Learning what makes a person truly happy may take some time, as will learning to trust the guidance from their inner voice.

Living a complete life is a journey within, to sift through the opinions of others and the negative self-talk you may have experienced throughout life. The intention is to find the truth of who you are. This journey is not about hardship or suffering. It is meant to be a positive learning experience with finding joy and inner self-love as the result. It is an opportunity for you to explore the world around you and recognize what is true and right for you. As this journey continues you will discover a life that has inner purpose and deep, personal meaning.

Some people would say because of the challenges they have faced, they do not have a connection with their inner purpose, or a life of deep personal meaning. What then?

When the challenges of a person's life are seen as learning experiences for positive growth, they begin to overcome any emotional trauma these experiences may have caused. This is the beginning of accepting responsibility for one's life.

Through the act of forgiveness, you release the people who cause your suffering from your consciousness. Forgiveness is the path to emotional healing and recognizing your inner purpose. There may have been painful experiences in your life, yet your inner self-love can ease your pain while you begin to experience a complete life. It is this inner love that moves you away from your painful experience toward a more loving, meaningful life.

Can I be hurt emotionally if I am living a complete life?

To live a complete life is to be emotionally strong, so the hurtful words or actions of others no longer affect you as they may have in your past. Why? Because you know the truth of who you are and you have found strength in the inner love you have for yourself. Also, you learn to understand the reasons why people behave as they do. Recognize that those who harm others are not connected to their true selves and are denying themselves their self-love through their negative behavior. You can forgive those who attempt to hurt you, while maintaining your emotions in a loving, caring manner. With your inner strength—found in living a complete life—you remain centered and focused on your self-love, while you do not allow the negative words or actions of others to offend you.

What about the people who cause pain to others? How do we avoid them?

All people have within them a source of inner guidance they must learn to trust. This inner guidance is always directing you to what is true and right. Guidance is received from the emotions and feelings you experience in any situation. While living a complete life, you quickly learn to trust these feelings as guidance. In your new awareness of this guidance, you know when you meet someone if they are trustworthy or not, or if a situation will become uncomfortable. The uncomfortable sensation is guidance. Acknowledge and then follow the guidance before the situation becomes stressful.

How often have you heard, "I had this funny feeling, yet I went ahead anyway." This "funny feeling" is your inner guidance telling you, you may want to reconsider your current actions, then move in a direction that makes you feel more comfortable. This guidance is there to prevent you from getting emotionally or physically hurt.

Living a complete life means you are learning to trust this guidance without doubt or hesitation. Your inner guidance is always directing you toward the best decisions and the safest places for you at all times. If the results of your choices do not work out as you had planned, it may be because you are not aware of the importance of this loving guidance.

Is trusting my emotions part of living a complete life?

Living a complete life is about discovering your true self and the guidance your emotions speak to you. A complete life is based on a desire to experience the joy of your true self-love. It is not founded in the self-centered need to prove yourself to yourself, or those around you. Your emotions are a reflection of what is going on within you as well as the world around you. If you are joyous and happy then this positive energy will be reflected back to you by the world around you. The opposite is also true. When you are angry or irritated, this energy will also be reflected back to you in how you perceive the world.

There is a fine line between experiencing my inner self-love and a life driven by my ego. How do I separate the two when it comes to living a complete life?

A boastful, ego-driven life is one spent searching for the approval or admiration of others. Though this kind of behavior may bring a small amount of happiness, it will never equal the deep, inner happiness found while experiencing your true, authentic self.

The fine line is a rather large gap which is felt easier than it can be explained. One way to tell the difference between a loving, compassionate life and one driven by the ego is by how you feel while engaged in one or the other. When you are living a complete life the validation you seek from the outside world will be found within you. There becomes no need to boast or brag about your accomplishments or your material possessions. In a complete life, the way you live your life will tell people who you truly are. A complete life is now found within you, not in the eyes of those you are trying to impress.

That's what makes this subject so powerful, "The validation I seek from the outside world will be found within me."

As you begin to live a complete life, you will not be asking those around you for validation or to boost your self-worth. You know what is right for you by how the thought of it makes you feel. This is where you learn to fully trust your inner guidance on many of the subjects you encounter throughout your day. As these changes begin, your inner voice becomes your guide to a meaningful life. From here, you begin to enjoy your inner self-love, a love no other person or relationship can equal.

Is it possible to have a loving relationship while living a complete life?

It will be unlike any relationship you have ever had. This is because once you know what makes you truly happy, on a deep inner level, you will not be asking your partner to behave or change who they are in a way that pleases you emotionally. You will be asking your partner to find their own inner joy and happiness as well, so the two of you can experience each other as honest, self-loving people.

Such a powerful thought, I will not be asking my partner to please me emotionally.

Your partner will naturally please you emotionally, as you will them. Yet they will do this because they love you, not because they feel it is their obligation to please you. Allowing each other to live an honest, authentic, complete life will bring each of you great joy.

If both people in a relationship are living complete lives, will there be less pressure to maintain the collective happiness of the relationship?

If both people in the relationship are living complete lives, there is no pressure to maintain the collective happiness. Each person will be living and experiencing their inner truth of self-love and self-compassion, then sharing this love and compassion with each moment together. While in this self-loving place there is no expectation for one person to make the other happy. Happiness is found within each individual. The pressure happens when one person is in need of the other person's love or approval, as a way to boost their self-worth. In a complete life, there is no need to ask this from the other person. Inner self-love will keep the relationship fresh and free from drama and uncertainty.

Many people build walls as a way to protect themselves emotionally from the pain they have suffered or may suffer. Is this necessary in order to live a complete life?

There is a belief that to experience one's true self, people must protect themselves from the outside world. This is a powerful false belief. Building walls as a way to safeguard oneself emotionally also blocks one's ability to feel love from the outside world.

A person will build emotional walls because they may be too afraid to begin the journey of discovering their authentic truth or forgive themselves for carrying the burden of a past emotional pain. Finding inner self-love does not mean to keep this love to oneself. When a person begins to experience a complete life, their inner love will be so strong they will want to share this love and compassion without condition, or expectation.

People who live a complete life realize their self-love and inner happiness are their responsibility, leaving others the responsibility for their own happiness. Though this may seem as if they need to isolate themselves from other people, this is not the case. Through experiencing inner joy they will be speaking and living this powerful truth. They will want to share this love and joy with all those they encounter throughout their day.

I am beginning to understand how living a complete life can be a powerful transformation for people.

Through this transformation, you will experience your inner self-love. This will change the way you view the world. As you share your true self-love, the world around you will respond to this love in positive ways.

For many, living a complete life may be the first time they are aware of the truth of who they are. At first this could be a challenge, but in a short amount of time, the comfort of being one's authentic self changes the way they experience the world, along with the way the world experiences them.

Living a complete life is so powerful the world around me will react in positive ways toward me?

Living a complete life is the realization that you are now connected with the truth of who you are. Because of this, you will be thinking, speaking, and living through the never-ending flow of love that is the foundation of your authentic self. The love and joy you have been seeking from others will now be found within you. You learn to trust yourself as you may never have before, thereby taking responsibility for your current life. The inner comfort of living a complete life will attract in to your life more positive, loving experiences from the people and the world around you.

How will living a complete life attract positive, loving experiences in to my life?

To live and speak your truth honestly, is the way people will experience who you are. Because of this, they will react to you with love and compassion. There will be no need for you to speak harshly or with anger toward other people. Your priority is to maintain your inner love, joy, and happiness, and then share this happiness with the people in your life. Living a complete life is knowing the truth of who you are, then giving this gift to the world.

My Final Thoughts

As I read this book once more, I realize there will never be a final thought or a final question. There is always going to be one more question and from there the answer will generate another question. Through these questions and answers, knowledge continues to expand. The joy I have experienced while writing this book has come from the never-ending wisdom spoken through my Inner Voice.

The present state of my life and this book came to be because I wanted more connection. A connection with what, I had no idea at the time. While writing this book and my daily journal writings, I have discovered what I was in search of was within me—true self-love. Each day I work at living my life through this love. I have learned this love is who I am, and this love is at the core of all humanity—which includes everyone, even you.

A complete life for me means that every thought, word, and action, originates from love. The choice is mine to accept this or not. I also know the outcome of my life will be dictated by this powerful choice. Every one of us has this same choice, though we can choose to believe this or not.

I am grateful for all the lessons that have helped me arrive at this point. These chapters have expanded my awareness of the love and wisdom found within me. Because of this, I share this love and wisdom with you, and those who are seeking a complete life.

I would like to thank you for picking up this book and continuing the journey to discover your authentic self. You will experience great love and many other benefits, as you begin the journey to live a complete life.

Acknowledgments

I have lived enough of life to recognize that nothing happens on its own. A tree grows with sunlight, fertile soil, and water. Writing a book is no different. There is input, feedback, edits, and modifications. Each step is intended to benefit the final outcome. I'm fortunate to have honest, supportive people in my life. As with my first book I appreciate the help I have received from many people along the way to publishing this one.

I begin with thanking my siblings, Lynne, Mark, and Marie. All of whom have been teaching me important lessons throughout my life. Their lessons helped shape the way I experience the world today. I am grateful to have them in my life.

I would like to thank Mike Fisher for his work helping me set up much of my internet presence. Mike speaks the language of the internet, which I do not. I appreciate his patience, understanding, and sense of humor when it comes to my language barrier.

When I first began querying articles, Krysta Gibson, publisher of *New Spirit Journal* was encouraging and supportive of my writing. Since then, she has been a champion for the Wisdom of My Inner Voice. For that I am grateful.

Every book needs an editor, Cielo Veda was there to help me through the first round of edits. I value her guidance, support, and positive input.

I appreciate the support of Elisa Tanaka for her creativity and her insightful work on the cover, Mary Dado for her editing skills and witty humor, and Tracey Kern, for our friendship and bi-weekly phone calls where we talk about books, writing, and beyond. Tracey is the driving force behind Conscious Shift Publishing, as well as being responsible for getting all the parts and pieces together to create this book. Thanks for all your help.

Through much of my life, I have had my lovely wife, Jane by my side. Her infinite wisdom, patience, and love have given me the courage to sort through the distractions of life to find the direction that is true and right for me. I'm fortunate to have such a loving partner on this journey.

About the Author

Author, blogger, and columnist, Paul Hudon resides with his wife, Jane, in a high mountain valley in Colorado where he finds inspiration for his books and articles. When not writing or working in their gardens, Paul takes advantage of the Colorado scenery by walking in the woods with Jane and their dogs, mountain biking, and riding his motorcycle.

Also by the author
Your Inner Guidance, The Path to Discovering Your True Happiness
published in 2021

Paul publishes a weekly blog and an e-newsletter, as well as contributing a monthly column for several online magazines.

For more information, or if you would like to contact Paul visit his website at:

PaulHudonAuthor.com

Your Thoughts

While writing in a journal I became aware of my inner voice. These pages are here for you to write your thoughts, so you can connect with your inner voice.

Relax, quiet your mind, and allow this loving voice to be heard.

NOTES

NOTES

Notes

Notes

NOTES

Notes

Notes

Notes

Notes

Notes

Made in the USA
Columbia, SC
24 May 2022